PUBLIC, TRADE UNION AND COOPERATIVE ENTERPRISE IN GERMANY

Public, Trade Union and Cooperative Enterprise in Germany

The Commonweal Idea

WALTER HESSELBACH

translated from the German by

KARL KÜHNE

FRANK CASS : LONDON

First published 1976 in Great Britain by
FRANK CASS AND COMPANY LIMITED
67 Great Russell Street, London WC1B 3BT, England

and in United States of America by
FRANK CASS AND COMPANY LIMITED
c/o International Scholarly Book Services Inc.
10300 S. W. Allen Boulevard, Beaverton, Oregon 97005

ISBN 0 7146 2978 2

Library of Congress Catalog No. 73-93194

Text set in 11 pt. Photon Times, printed by photolithography
and bound in Great Britain at The Pitman Press, Bath

Contents

Preface to the English Edition

West Germany has had a Social Democratic Government for several years now, and left wing German student activity is reported in the English press from time to time, yet the conventional image of West Germany held by the Anglo-Saxon reader is that of an entirely private enterprise economy producing economic miracles. This book is a welcome antidote to this view, for it brings to our attention those elements in the German economy which are not profit-motivated or which are not privately owned. It traces those ideas of economists and political philosophers which have been influential in the development of these elements, sets down the history of the organizations and outlines a theory of the role which they might play today.

For the English reader the book has two major merits. It provides the first account in English of the development in Germany of non-profit oriented bodies such as consumer cooperatives, insurance companies, workers' banks and the "Bank für Gemeinwirtschaft", and secondly it gives an indication of the state of debate in Germany about non-profit making, public or cooperatively owned institutions.

The reader will be struck by the use of the unusual term "commonweal" both as adjective and noun. This usage is deliberate, since "commonweal" is a close counterpart for the German "Gemeinwirtschaft". It is Herr Hesselbach's aim in Germany to proselytize on behalf of cooperative, non-profit oriented and publicly-owned organizations and to this end he uses the compendious term "Gemeinwirtschaft". In English he wishes to advance his ideas under the heading of "commonweal". There are many precedents for this in intellectual history; schools of writers have been designated by such assorted terms as "Encyclopédistes", "Mercantilists" and "Utilitarians" to name but three from a range of possible examples.

R. Shaw
University of Aberdeen

Terminological Note

To begin with, let me quote that malicious Italian proverb: "Traduttore—traditore!" ("Translator = Traitor"!). In fact, whoever wants to render a sophisticated author's terms in the right way, had better use a roundabout expression. We may compare individual words with circles; in two different languages, even if the meaning seems to be more or less the same, two of these circles will never coincide exactly and will sometimes just touch each other. The situation is even worse whenever there is no complete agreement on the meaning of the term in the respective languages. This is certainly the case with the term "Gemeinwirtschaft": within the last century at least four different interpretations have been proffered.

First of all, there is the so-called "dualistic" interpretation: according to this point of view, "Gemeinwirtschaft" is just the antithesis of "market economy", apt to "correct" or to complement it. The market economy consists of firms following the principles of private business: maximization of profits, or at least realization of a certain minimum of profitability. If private business has its full sway, there is the danger that certain kinds of wants will not be satisfied, or that "social costs" will be exorbitant, unless other kinds of enterprise or institutions interfere which do not adhere to the profit principle, primarily. This was the interpretation offered by the German economist and philosopher Schäffle, in the last quarter of the nineteenth century, and it has been further developed by an authority on Public Finance, Professor Ritschl of Hamburg University.

On the other side of the picture, there is the "monistic" interpretation, based upon the idea that "Gemeinwirtschaft" represents a principle that is completely alien or repugnant to the principle of the market economy; adherents to this idea speak of public enterprise as "alien elements" ("Fremdkörper"). According to this thesis, "Gemeinwirtschaft" should be a synonym of a "centrally administered economic system", or of an administrative system or "planned system" in the general sense of the word. Some writers have even treated the two terms "Gemeinwirtschaft" and "socialism" as synonyms. It is for this reason that the title of the most important book written by one of the chief protagonists of this thesis, the liberal-minded Professor Ludwig von Mises—"Gemeinwirtschaft"—has been rendered in English as "Socialism".

There is a third version which might be described as the "theory of dominance" or "dominant Gemeinwirtschaft". Its protagonists hold that the principle of "Gemeinwirtschaft" is progressing, first because in modern times community tasks are growing in comparison with private tasks or tasks which can be solved by private enterprise, and secondly because the principle of "Gemeinwirtschaft" might be inherently superior to the principle of private business. It is true that the defenders of this thesis do not claim that the principle of "Gemeinwirtschaft" ought to comprise the whole of our economic life; however, they think that, under present circumstances, it might be desirable to extend its sphere. The chief representative of this idea, the great German authority on Public Finance, Adolf Wagner, formulated the so-called "law of growth of State activity", in this context.

The fourth tendency which is at present gaining more and more ground, proposes a "pluralistic" version of the notion of "Gemeinwirtschaft". According to this formula, a multitude of enterprises or institutions may act in a manner corresponding to the principle of "Gemeinwirtschaft", in so far as they are the property of public bodies or of any institution working according to the principle of "Gemeinwirtschaft", provided they are really acting on the basis of that principle. This fourth group more or less equates the two terms of "gemeinwirtschaftlich" and "gemeinnützig" (in the interest of the community, "public utility"); it stands in a close relation to the "dualism" of the first group, but it holds that a great number of units or enterprises making decisions would not only be possible, but should be considered desirable, not only in the case of private enterprise, but also in public and cooperative enterprise and in general in the sector of what may be called "gemeinwirtschaftlich". This opinion is put forward by Gerhard Weisser, an Emeritus Professor of Cologne University, and his disciple Dr. Thiemeyer.

It is now of paramount importance, as far as the translator is concerned, which interpretation he wants to render by the terms he chooses. It may seem that the second interpretation could easily be translated. However, one should not render it simply by "socialism" or "socialisme", in French, for this term does not do justice to the idea one wants to convey, and it may again be interpreted in many different ways. It would be better to employ the terms "State Economy" or "Administrative Economy", in French "Economie étatique" or "Economie administrée". The three other terms are certainly closer to each other; it will nevertheless be possible to distinguish between them.

As the first interpretation only confronts two different economic sectors, it will be best to render it in English by talking of the "private sector" and the "public sector". It is true that the term does not render exhaustively the meaning of the word "gemeinwirtschaftlicher Bereich". It would thus be necessary to find some complementary term. Nevertheless, this antithesis may also be applied to the third interpretation. It is the fourth interpretation which furnishes the complement. First of all, it is of no avail to use the term "gemeinnützig", because it carries a different connotation in other languages, being primarily a lawyer's term; for instance, it will have to be rendered in French by "sans but lucratif" and in English by "public utility". The language of the EEC treaty is also largely juridical: in article 90 of the Treaty Rome, paragraph 2, the legislator talks about "services of general economic interest", translating the term by "intérêt économique général" (in French) and "interesse economico generale" (Italian), which would correspond to "interés económico general" in Spanish and "general economic interest" in English. These formulations certainly come very near to the German term, as well as the French term "service public", but they are all too vague in English.

Some people tried to get round these difficulties by introducing the term "collective economy" ("économie collective" in French). This translation contains two disadvantages. First, in the realm of Public Finance, the term "collective wants" means something quite different, namely a bundle of individual wants running parallel to each other. Besides, the term implies the "collectivist" totalitarian system as it is practised in some Eastern countries. Yet we ought to choose a term that is completely devoid of any ideological ambiguity. Moreover, the term has another subsidiary meaning in English: "collective enterprises"—for instance, in the sense as used by Robson—are those that belong to several local authorities or public authorities at a higher level collectively, i.e. joint public enterprise, as in the case of Belgian so-called "intercommunales". But we do not want to talk about establishments belonging to several authorities at the same time, when talking about "collective enterprise". For all these reasons, CIRIEC has dropped the term "collective economy" in English and chosen the translation "Public and cooperative enterprise". This, however, seems to be too cumbersome a term, and anyway it cannot be used as an adjective. At any rate, it seems to be absolutely indispensable to use a single-word expression in English.

In a volume containing several reprinted articles recently edited by Peacock and Musgrave (*Classics of the Theory of Public Finance*, New York, 1967, page 233), an article by Professor Ritschl has been reprinted, and its title "Gemeinwirtschaft" is rendered by "Communal Economy". This does not seem to be a very happy solution either. First of all, we thus have an adjective, but no proper noun; and secondly, the term "communal", according to the *Concise Oxford Dictionary* (1964), means "of a commune, of the Paris commune, of the antagonistic religious and racial communities", and "communalism" demotes the "theory of government by local autonomy", i.e. the sector of local authorities. This is not what we want to express when talking of "Gemeinwirtschaft", and least of all do we want to say anything that implies the "Paris Commune" or racial disturbances in this context . . .

However, there is another term in English which, it is true, the *Oxford Dictionary* qualifies as "archaic", and which is seldom used in its original meaning, but which may be revived just because it is no longer being used currently; this is the term "commonweal". A fine distinction has to be made between the same term written separately in two words or in one word. This term originally derives from the root "wealth", and it may also be interpreted as meaning "common property". On the other hand, the element of "public welfare" is indubitably represented in this term, which thus means anything that may be good for the community as a whole. If we use the term in its single-word form, this will have the advantage that it can also be employed as an adjective. We therefore propose to use the term "commonweal" in English to render the German word "Gemeinwirtschaft".

In the past the term "commonweal" was used as a synonym of "commonwealth". The *Oxford Dictionary* still indicates for both terms the meaning "public welfare". We may also quote the *Dictionary of the Social Sciences*, edited by J. Gould and W. L. Kolb (London 1964), which states on page 110: "The term began as a synonym for public welfare . . . It meant: a) the common good, b) a free community organized for the principle of the common good . . ."

This second interpretation seems to coincide rather precisely with the "pluralistic" interpretation of the term "gemeinwirtschaftliche Unternehmung (enterprise) oder Organisation" in German.

In this sense, the term existed already in the seventeenth century, as it is mentioned in W. K. Hancock's text "A very and true Comyn Wele" (reprinted in *Politics in Pitcairn*, London 1947, p. 95). Gould and Kolb, in their *Dictionary of the Social Sciences* (p. 110) declare, with regard to this second meaning (b): "In the second of these senses, the word was used as an alternative for State, but always with distinct overtones of public benefit". Today the term has practically become a synonym of "State" or "Association of States", in the form of "Commonwealth", or it means "body politic", e.g. in Australia, or "republic" (Cromwell); thus, the term "commonwealth" has acquired a different meaning and can no longer be used.

All this justifies the proposal to use the more ancient term "commonweal". In this context, we may also mention the term "common good". This term has been used in an extensive sense by H. Green in his work *Principles of Political Obligation* (London 1913); it has a certain affinity to the term "public benefit" or "public interest". However, the latter terms seem to coincide rather more with the German terms "Allgemeinwohl" or "Allgemeininteresse", and their use cannot be recommended.

Foreword

This book is intended to provide a survey of the history, the theory and the activities of the most important commonweal enterprises of the German workers' movement and of the German consumers' cooperative societies. There are two reasons for publishing such a book: first of all, there is an interest in the topic at the political level, and secondly, there is the desire to stimulate scientific discussion.

The political reason for publishing such a book is that since the enterprises under discussion have reached a size large enough to pursue their commonweal objectives with vigour, they have been attacked again and again at the political level. Critics declare that economic power is a menace in the hands of trade union "bureaucrats" and of managers of cooperative societies.

It is quite clear that successful and active enterprises belonging to trade unions and to consumers' cooperative societies constitute a new nucleus of power. It is their rôle to provide what Galbraith calls "countervailing power". Power in itself is nothing we need detest. It is always a matter of concern to what ends the power is used, and whether such power can be controlled by law in the interest of democracy.

In fact, economic discussion is now focussing on the business enterprises of trade unions and consumers' cooperative societies, because of their commonweal aims and successes. They are being attacked because of their increasing effectiveness in promoting the interests of large groups of consumers. This book should make this clear and should describe the conditions under which these enterprises are operating in the public interest in their markets.

At the same time this book should stimulate scientific work in politics and history. A comprehensive survey of trade union enterprises and of consumers' cooperative societies is still lacking. It should be recalled that the social movement began in the 19th century with the foundation of commonweal enterprise, that there followed the culture orientated organizations of the German workers' movement and the trade unions, and that the workers' parties, about which so much is written in historical and political work, were the last of the four "pillars" of the workers' movement. There is an ample literature on consumers' cooperative societies, but in spite of their long history hardly a coherent text exists on the enterprises of the German workers' movement.

Last but not least economists, and particularly industrial economists, should be reminded of the fact that these enterprises are very important for economic theory. Fundamentally important from the point of view of what is called in Germany "morphology of the firm" (theory of industrial structure) they are also important for competition policy and for growth policy, their significance in this last sphere arising from the enlargement of the infrastructure.

This book is a new and enlarged edition of the book published in 1966 on the subject of commonweal enterprise. Apart from the enlargement and the insertion of complementary texts, the present book is based on a paper delivered to the Academy "Kontakte der Kontinente" (Contacts between Continents) and which was later published as part of a Festscrift in honour of Prof. Gert von Eynern. Another contribution to a Festschrift in honour of Prof-Dr. Bruno Gleitze has been incorporated into the text, as has a paper delivered to the "Verein zur Förderung der Gemeinwirtschaft" (Association for the Furthering of Commonweal Economy) at Hamburg.

I have to thank Dr. Achim von Loesch, who has carried out preparatory work for the final edition of this book. For the last ten years he has been helping me to develop commonweal theory and to publish articles and books on this subject.

It is only because of his assistance that I have been able, despite full-scale business activities, to formulate my ideas on this subject. I have also to thank the division "Gemeinwirtschaft (Commonweal Economy) for their reading of the proofs, and the publisher "Europäische Verlagsanstalt", who looked after the indexes for persons and subject matter, as well as Dr. Kühne (Brussels) and Mr. Robert Shaw, Lecturer (Department of Political Economy, King's College, University of Aberdeen), who revised the English translation.

PART I

History and Analysis of the Discussion on Commonweal Economy

Chapter 1

COMMONWEAL ECONOMY AS A NEW ECONOMIC ORDER

Since the end of the reconstruction period after the Second World War, new solutions to economic and social problems have been under discussion, for the possibilities contained in old theories and conditions inherited have mostly been exhausted. In this context the old question has been re-examined as to whether and how far the ideas of a commonweal order in economic life and of commonweal forms of enterprise are really useful and practicable. The dominant idea of the reconstruction period was that the only possible way to improve living standards lay in organizing the economy on the lines of private enterprise with economic life directed to the pursuit of profit in a market system. This was largely a reaction to the planned economy of the war period. In many cases these ideas also resulted from pure resignation, because other solutions did not appear to be possible or desirable.

In the meantime these tendencies have receded. It is once more accepted that things can be done otherwise, the more so as industrial countries have been confronted increasingly with the industrialization of developing countries. In the latter new configurations of spiritual, social and political forces are appearing, which are completely different from those still existing in industrial countries. These new forces also differ from systems prevailing about 100 to 150 years ago, when Europe was becoming industrialized. In addition modern economics and social sciences provide tools to examine all eventualities and to control the social systems existing in industrial countries. In particular the progress of modern social sciences has created a growing readiness to accept new possibilities.

All this makes possible a new and wider discussion of the subject, commonweal economy. Preparatory scientific work has been set afoot. The question of what constitutes commonweal aims has been re-examined from a methodological point of view. The realization of actual aims and tasks has made it possible to redeem the postulate about supra-individual goals from the odium of empty nominality (1). It has also been proved that commonweal economy is a precondition for the workability of the private sector. Experience, especially in commonweal enterprises of the German workers' movement, has shown the functional workability of commonweal enterprise as an instrument for the fulfilment of certain economic tasks (2).

At the same time important elements, which had been associated with the earlier discussion of commonweal enterprise, have become, under different names, recognized tools of economics.

It is now possible to give a comprehensive survey of the field of commonweal economy and to discuss it with a wider and more interested public. In doing so we must start from the fact that there are three different versions of the term "commonweal economy" in the German language. First of all, there is understood by "Gemeinwirtschaft" an economic system of a special character. This is what we call the "monistic" concept. Secondly, "Gemeinwirtschaft" may mean the public sector, i.e. whole sectors of the economy that are under the control of the state or of municipalities. This is the "dualistic" concept.

Finally, the term "Gemeinwirtschaft" may be used to cover cooperative societies and commonweal enterprises, which belong to trade unions. This is the pluralistic concept of "Gemeinwirtschaft". The fact that one single word is used in different ways inhibits understanding. In what follows the term "Gemeinwirtschaft" (which we render by "commonweal economy") is examined in detail, and a proposed solution to the terminological problem is offered.

"COMMONWEAL ECONOMY" – CENTRALLY CONTROLLED ECONOMY

The concept "commonweal economy", as an economic system, i.e. the "monistic" sense of "Gemeinwirtschaft", is only rarely used in the economic literature of our times (3). By this term is understood mainly a closed economic system without markets or competition, wherein everything is regulated according to the aims, which have been fixed by the political authorities. This interpretation of the term "Gemeinwirtschaft" covers very old economic systems and very modern ones: the state economy of ancient times, the great planning systems of both world wars, and the centrally administered economic systems of the socialist blocks today.

In the 19th century the ideas of such an alternative to the market economy based on private property had been propagated by economists belonging to the historical school in their opposition to the so-called Manchester school. These economists were still relying on certain traditions in Germany, on what is called "cameralism" as well as on mercantilism, and they pointed out the important rôle of the public factor in economic life. They had also shown that in economic life, beside the pursuit of profits for the individual, supra-individual aims as well were being pursued. These economists had coined the comprehensive term of "Gemeinwirtschaft" = "commonweal economy" for all business units, sectors or economic systems based upon the principle of the common good, no matter whether they were dealing with single households, enterprises or economic systems.

The notion of "Gemeinwirtschaft" ("commonweal economy") was introduced into the economic literature by Friedrich Benedict Wilhelm von Hermann (1795–1868), one of the most important representatives of the classical school of economics in Germany. He pointed out that economic life was not just a matter of private persons, that not all firms, and least of all the state, followed the principle of maximizing profits, and that there were many undertakings following the principle of the common good (4). The British classical economists had not questioned the applicability of the profit motive to all individual firms. Hermann, however, asserted that this principle could not be automatically applied to all economic agents. Wilhelm Roscher, the founder of the historical school of economics (1817–1894), pointed out later that this particular reasoning did not apply only to private households, but also to the municipal and state economy (5). Albert Schäffle (1831–1903), in the last edition of his most important book, enlarged the idea of commonweal economy and applied it to the whole economic system. He envisaged a monistic commonweal system, a "rational social state" with money certificates based on labour, public property and planning (6).

The collapse of the world economy during the First World War, the militarization of economic life and the propagation of the principle of autarky, as well as the introduction of elements of a centrally administered system, gave rise to a large wave of commonweal literature and plans between 1914 and 1924. These works were influenced by the experiences of large combines, by corporative and socialist ideas, and by a kind of "War-time Socialism" (7).

The article regarding public ownership in the Constitution of Weimar, the demands for public ownership in many party programmes and also the demand for a planned economy were all more or less dependent on this discussion. War-time socialist ideas were partly of a corporative character (in that they envisaged the retention of private property with regard to means of production, the organization of the economic system in firms and corporations, and the subjection of the whole economy to the will of the community – as was the case with W. Rathenau, R. Wissel, W. v. Moellendorf), and they also partly envisaged a totally socialist planning system with exchange in kind (O. Neurath, K. Ballod) (8).

In both cases roughly sketched projects of a socialist character were developed, which soon provoked the criticism of professional economists. The best-known critique by a liberal author is the book *Die Gemeinwirtschaft* (*The Commonweal Economy*) by Ludwig von Mises (9). His analysis was continued by F. A. Hayek and W. Röpke. It all boiled down to a rather single-minded emphasis on the market economy based upon private property, and to the affirmation that rational economic behaviour was only possible in such a market economy. A comprehensive discussion on planning finally led to a result which was, paradoxically, the opposite of the critical attacks launched by Mises and Hayek.

The up-shot of this discussion on rational economic calculation in a planned economic system, or, as was said in those days, commonweal system, was a partial recognition on both sides of the validity of the adversaries' thesis. Ludwig von Mises had to swallow the reproach that the possibility of rational economic activity in a planned system had long before been proved by Enrico Barone (in 1908) (10). The liberal authors had to recognize that a capitalist system based upon private property and free competition is not the only rational and efficient system in the world. They also had to admit the possibility of a more or less strictly organized economic system based on the satisfaction of wants. The socialists for their part (E. Heimann, C. Landauer, E. Lederer), had to recognize the importance of the individual's right to freedom, viz. freedom of consumption based on the existence of free markets. They had to accept the function of the free market, viz. to bring about economic order, and they recognized that capitalism and the free market economy were not necessarily synonymous.

The debate of the twenties about the economic calculus in planned economies and market economies led to such an amount of agreement in both camps, that after the Second World War the market system was accepted by both sides, despite the fact that the Second World War had also started a debate on planning and socialism, which found its reflection in certain articles of the constitution. A further result was that the discussion led to a general recognition of the principle of the market system, and the only problem, which remained to be solved, was the extent to which central elements of order and administration should come into being.

Today the systems, which are grouped under the term of centrally planned economy, are in many cases not seen as alternatives to a market system. It has been recognized that we are dealing with two different and competing principles of control, which coexist to different degrees in any economic system. These are the principles of a centrally planned economic life, in most cases conducted by the government, and of the decentralization of economic life into the hands of individual producers and consumers.

It is not necessarily true that these two competing systems of control exclude each other. The thesis that both types have a tendency to appear in pure forms is no longer accepted. On the contrary economists now recognize that it is not true that only the two extreme types are stable and that mixed systems are unstable. They have discovered that, on the contrary, the mixed types are stable and the pure ones are in fact unstable. In Western countries the issue in practice is concerned only with one particular point, i.e. how many planned elements have to be introduced into a decentralized system, in principle, to serve as elements of order and incentive, and what are the ways and means by which these planning interventions are to be carried out, so as to make sure that the mixed system will function in the best possible way. In the Eastern block the question at the moment is where, how and to what degree should decentralized elements of control be introduced, in principle, into a system, which is directed from the centre.

COMMONWEAL ECONOMY – PUBLIC ENTERPRISE

The term "Gemeinwirtschaft" is, however, still being used in a second dualistic version, as a synonym for public enterprise. In this sense the term "commonweal economy" comprises all business concerns, which are the property of public authorities.

During the 19th century German economists protested against the liberalism of the Manchester school, a protest chiefly based upon moral considerations and romantic ideas. They were repulsed by the dance round the "Golden Calf", and they emphasized that in reality not all business units followed private aims and the principle of profit maximization. These ideas together with the development of modern transport systems and public utilities, afforded them a new political insight; that to function efficiently the capitalist economic system required a framework of economic units, which did not have the motivation of private firms. The most outspoken protagonist of the idea of commonweal enterprise as a base and a framework for private enterprise was the so-called "armchair socialist" Adolph Wagner (1835–1917) (11). Ever since, commonweal economy has been advocated as a system of public enterprise complementary to the private market economy. The theory of a dualistic commonweal and private economic system has been further developed and enlarged by Margit Cassel (12), Hans Ritschl (13) and Alfred Ammon (14).

In the last decade the idea that private business requires a commonweal or public framework has again come to the forefront. With the new insight the terms have simultaneously been changed, in the same way as in the discussion about the economic system. Since then the discussion about the importance and the extent of economic activity, which is not to be administered according to private-enterprise principles, has been conducted through the term "infrastructure", which has been borrowed from military strategy. In this context enterprises, which are absolutely necessary as a basis for the workability of private enterprise, are referred to as "infrastructure enterprises".

This return to the idea of a general commonweal framework necessary for the economic system has been a consequence of the high rates of growth together with the reconstruction of the West German economy and its reintegration into the world trading system. It has been demonstrated that a high rate of growth of private production and private consumption necessitates a more than proportional enlargement of the infrastructure. Since then this idea has entered into all party programmes. Differences between conservative and progressive groups in Germany on this question only consist of the fact that conservative elements are demanding, somewhat unwillingly, an enlargement of the infrastructure parallel to the development of private economy, whereas progressive groups welcome the new infrastructure investment and want it to precede the growth of the private sector, thereby stimulating this sector. In so doing, the progressive groups can appeal to modern growth theories in economics from which the new economic concept has been derived. Modern growth theories add to full-employment theory the postulate of a satisfactory rate of economic growth, and they prove that the enlargement of the infrastructure is a condition and an instrument of policy for full-employment and growth. By anticipating investment in the infrastructure, the growth of the economy may be regulated in such a way that full capacity use can be attained at all times.

The demand for socialism put forward in the period immediately after both world wars and aimed at the nationalization of certain parts of the economic system, has been dropped in the meantime. These demands envisaged a forcible transfer of entire economic sectors into public or commonweal ownership. On one side this was considered to be the beginning of a full-scale nationalization of the economic system, while on the other it was thought to be applicable only to the key-industries of the economy. After the Second World War in particular it had only been considered necessary to transfer the key industries into public ownership. That the demands for public ownership of particular parts of the economy contained elements of war-time socialism could be seen not only from the strength of these demands after both great wars, but was particularly obvious from the fact that the industries such proposals aimed at were key industries producing raw materials and energy. The demands for public ownership and the concept of a key industry were both influenced by the years of privation, during and immediately after the war years, when raw materials and energy were scarce.

Similar generalizations from particular instances of time and periods of shortages have led to the claim that banks should be nationalized. In Germany the situation was different from that prevailing in England or France for during industrialization, money and capital had mostly been scarce, so that there was considerable hostility regarding the power of the banks from the German middle-class, and this hostility also entered into political programmes. Political parties of the left and trade unions soon desisted from emphasizing their original demands to turn such sectors into public property. They quietly renounced these points of their programmes long before oil, atomic energy and artificial fibres deprived the traditional basic industries of their key-position, and before the instruments at the disposal of the central bank limited the power of private banks. The more the demand for public ownership receded, the more other demands receded, which aimed at making of the market economy a planned one.

Nevertheless, the trends aimed at nationalization and based on the idea of economic democracy were not dropped completely. The two groups of questions fundamental to socialism, viz. the problem of power and the problem of the distribution of the assets of growing enterprises lost their close link with the questions of property. From now on each of these questions was treated individually, in political discussion, under the headings of joint control and formation of capital.

It would be appropriate, from the point of view of modern economics, to disentangle the term "Gemeinwirtschaft" from the question of ownership and to cease to equate it with public enterprise. The contrast between private and public enterprise is of no importance for our discussion. It would be more fruitful, instead, to distinguish between the functions of business concerns in the process of production and the aims, which they are pursuing. Such a discussion based upon operational questions whould no longer focus on public enterprise and its problems, but would concentrate on the problems of banking, transportation, energy and other basic industries, and it would distinguish between business concerns in these fields according to the aims they were pursuing, dividing them into two groups, viz. the group of commonweal enterprise and the group of enterprises following the principles of private enterprise.

Chapter 2

COMMONWEAL ECONOMY AS A TERM OF INDUSTRIAL STRUCTURE

The pluralistic term commonweal economy must be distinguished from the two other types, the monistic and the dualistic type, not only from a quantitative point of view, for it has more forms, but also qualitatively as it is a term of micro-economics. Economic science developed two types of models: macro-economic models, which establish certain economic relationships for entire societies, and micro-economic models, which apply to individual business units and deal with the centres of power and of decision-making (15). By this systematization the rules are established by which individual participants in the economy cooperate, and in addition the institutions, by means of which individual economic units arrange their activities, are described.

The term commonweal enterprise has been used in both kinds of model, in the macro-economic sense as well as at the micro-economic level. The monistic term, viz. commonweal economy as a monolithic economic system, belongs to the group of macro-economic models of economic systems. Formerly the identification of commonweal economy and public economy also constituted a type of macro-economics. Public enterprises had, originally, been considered within the framework of commonweal discussion as being parts of a dualistic system and even as parts of or as the beginnings of a socialist system. Then the primarily individualistic outlook prevailed for some time. Meanwhile the tendency has grown to consider these enterprises again from a macro-economic viewpoint within the framework of the discussion on infrastructure. The pluralistic notion of commonweal economy, however, belongs unmistakably to the group of micro-economic models. In this case even cooperative and the so-called "free commonweal enterprise" belong to the commonweal sector, or to commonweal enterprise.

COOPERATIVE SOCIETIES

The cooperative society is together with public enterprise the oldest type of modern enterprise which is not profit-oriented. During the 19th century cooperative societies were proposed and fostered by conservatives as well as by socialists. Both saw them as the prototype of an enterprise of the future, which would no longer be profit-motivated. The first and best-known proposals for an alternative to the capitalist system aimed at a cooperative transformation of the entire economic system. Early socialists at the beginning of the 19th century had protested against the pessimism of classical economics, which accepted mass misery as the inevitable concomitant to industrialization.

The early socialists wanted to replace the private economic system by a commonweal system, an economic system with a new content, "which would no longer be based on private enterprise and on the division of the product between entrepreneurs and workers, but upon the fact of production being carried on by cooperative societies" (16). The two traditions, from which the protests of the early socialists stemmed, were Christian chiliasm and the social optimism of utopian writers and planners. These Christian and chiliastic circles referred to the communities of the early Christians, who lived in common cooperative households, held common property and were waiting for the Last Judgement and the return of their Saviour (17). This combination of Chiliasm and communist and cooperative community systems had been the basis of almost all revolutionary streams in Europe for 2,000 years (18).

Utopian writers, utopian planners and economists developed, partly on this basis and partly on the basis of the ideas of Encyclopaedic Enlightenment, complete models of an ideal society and of a just economic system, in nearly all cases based upon cooperative societies. In this group, we find Thomas More's *Utopia*, Bacon's *Atlantis*, Campanella's *The City of the Sun*, Andrea's *Christenstaat* (*State of the Christians*), Winstanley's *Law of Freedom*, Harrington's *Oceana*, d'Allais' *Sevarambes*, and the ideas of Zierikzee, Bellers, Robert Owen and of the early French socialists ranging from St. Simon to Proudhon, and further Morelly's *Code of Nature*, Cabet's *Icarian Voyage*, Morris's *New Utopia* and the ideas of Hertzka and Oppenheimer. It is an imposing array containing many famous names (10).

These books in the form of novels were followed by the founding, on a cooperative basis, of a considerable number of colonies or enterprises, which underwent a twofold process of differentiation during the 19th century. In the beginning these experiments embraced primitive and Utopian Communism, the colonies and communities being founded to comprehend all facets of human existence. These ad hoc realizations of an ideal society in small model communities were primitive, because they wanted to introduce common property not only with regard to the means of production but also with regard to the consumption of goods. Each individual was severely rationed in his consumption of goods (20).

This dream of equality through Communism had already occurred in the pre-industrial period. Many early socialists, therefore, refer to mediaeval prototypes, to monasteries, to communities of Baptists and to other ways of life, in which many sects had organized themselves. Reference can also be made to the most successful and, at the same time, fantastic experiment of Christian paternalistic Communism of a pre-industrial brand, viz. to the Jesuits' State in Paraguay. Again, the socialist colonies of the 19th century, founded in the spirit of Encyclopaedic Enlightenment, were often cooperative communities, which embraced all aspects of life and property. They followed primarily educational and cultural aims. The idea was that new men should be educated under new conditions free of exploitation and misery.

Among such foundations, which were carried out partly in the Christian spirit, and partly in the spirit of the Encyclopaedic Enlightenment and which were partly pre-industrial, and partly industrial, are numbered the colonies in Delaware and Pennsylvania, run along the lincs of the proposals of Zierikzee, Robert Owen's "New Harmony" in Indiana, and Queenswood in Hampshire in Great Britain. There were, besides, numerous phalansteries, which had been founded by Considérant and Godin, followers of Fourier. In Texas alone there were more than twenty-five of these and more than forty altogether in the United States. All these foundations foundered for very different reasons; Godin's "Familisterum" was the only successful phalanstery. It existed for more than forty years and numbered more than 2,000 members.

Utopias are visions of the future, with the intention of creating a better world. Since the writing of Bloch's book *Prinzip Hoffnung* (*The Principle of Hope*) (21), people in Germany have again become familiar with the notion of Utopia. In our century the Utopia of Zionism has been realized in the State of Israel. We witness men travelling to the moon; mankind must today realize its greatest dream of world peace, if it does not want to destroy itself one day. Unrealistic though the models of the early socialists may have been, nevertheless, they spurred on some action, whereas the Romantic writers, the other anti-capitalist stream of this period in the conservative camp, contributed only towards an idealization of the past, and shed new light on social development.

In the 19th century non-capitalist enterprise could only be conceived of in the form of cooperative societies. Socialists as well as conservatives arrogated to themselves the cooperative form of enterprise: liberals and socialists, because they considered that the principles of the Great French Revolution were realized in it, and conservatives and reactionary elements, because they wanted to recreate the good old days of the guilds and the corporate state.

Robert Owen, who had rediscovered the cooperative society, wanted to use it to eliminate the misery of the workers. Cooperative societies organized by Schulze-Delitzsch and Raiffeisen followed the principle of self-help amongst artisans and peasants in an attempt to defend them against the new claims of industry. In the eyes of all anti-capitalist forces of the 19th century this form of enterprise, the cooperative society, had the character of a social saviour. It was conceived as overcoming all past, present and future evil, by reconciling principles, which were considered to be incompatible, viz. freedom and order, the interests of the employed and the employers. Cooperative societies today still pursue aims of social reform. A leading theoretician of cooperation, Helmut Faust, characterizes cooperative societies as "social forms for the realization of a higher style of economic activity" (22). In the statutes of the International Cooperative Alliance of September, 1966, the intention to carry out reforms is proclaimed in paragraph 1. This reads as follows: "The International Cooperative Alliance . . . aims to replace the economic system based upon aspirations of profit, with a cooperative system, built upon the interests of the community and upon self-help" (23).

The transition from Utopian cooperative ideas to realistic ideas of reform, such as those contained in the statutes of the International Cooperative Alliance, took place in several stages. The social or religious colonies or communities based on cooperative principles lost more and more of their communist traits in the course of time and were replaced by cooperative business units of the productive type. The productive society no longer covered, as the Utopian colony did, the private or family life of its members. Religious and educational aims were pushed into the background. The society dealt primarily with economic emancipation. Alongside it, consumers', credit and housing societies were established.

The secularized cooperative movement soon comprised middle-class and peasant elements, progressively losing its political and anti-capitalist character. It no longer pursued the aim of overthrowing capitalism, but helped the middle-classes to adapt to the industrial system. Industrial cooperative societies created the possibility for important non-industrial groups to adapt to modern conditions. Nevertheless, the cooperative society, even in its simple form as a mutual aid institution, has remained of a primarily non-business and reformist nature up to the present.

THE COMPREHENSIVE COOPERATIVE SYSTEM

The Rochdale weavers and Schulze-Delitzsch had cherished the idea of a cooperative system embracing the whole of society, but, after many attempts to realize it, this idea had to be dropped. In Germany, the term "Gemeinwirtschaft" ("commonweal economy") had been coined by conservative economists for this notion. The protagonists of this idea, however, never succeeded in forming such an economic system within the framework of cooperation. There were various reasons for this failure. Firstly a cooperative business structure suitable for productive enterprises and owned by its workers was still lacking. Secondly, it was not possible to invent an appropriate clearing system for payments between cooperative enterprises at different levels of production.

What happened was that only particular sectors, for instance marketing, housing, savings and credit activities were organized according to cooperative principles, but these sectors could never be united within a "cooperative Commonwealth", as this system had been christened in England by the Fabian writers, Sidney and Beatrice Webb. (24) In Germany, the idea of a complete system based upon consumers' cooperative societies had been conceived much earlier, in 1869, by Eduard Pfeiffer (25). In France, the same idea had been advocated by Charles Gide and his Nîmes school (26). Gide argued that the entire economic system could be transformed into a system of consumers' cooperative societies. Local or regional consumers' societies would form secondary cooperatives at a higher level, which would organize the remaining process of distribution, until finally the entire system of production including agriculture was organized in this way.

In economics this concept has been dubbed "cooperation". It denotes a system of cooperation and mutual collaboration, which is finally to penetrate the entire society, and which is intended to overcome the commercial-capitalist system. Shortly before and after the First World War this concept of "cooperation" was propagated in Germany by Robert Wilbrandt, who thought that it would lead to a solution of all social and political problems (27).

The same idea in a somewhat watered-down form was taken up later by Fritz Naphtali, (28) and immediately after the Second World War it was again proposed by Henry Everling (29) in order to reform and correct an otherwise predominantly private enterprise system. Ernst Grünfeld, who had been one of the leading cooperators in the twenties, wrote that this "cooperation" or "cooperative Socialism" based on consumers' cooperative societies, was the only mature theory of a new community, which could claim to be of some scientific importance (30).

Almost all cooperative societies could look back on considerable successes not only in their educational efforts, but also in their contributions to the policy aimed at sound economic structures and at the maintenance of competition. In the agrarian sphere, agricultural credit cooperatives eliminated the greatest evil of the money economy, the private usurer. Agricultural buying and selling societies reduced the market status and thus the economic power of private dealers by offering effective competition. Traders' and artisans' cooperative societies could also look back upon similar successes. Cooperative societies have been successful in the border areas between pre-industrial and industrial activities, and have fulfilled a useful function for particular sectors and groups of people. The consumers' cooperative societies of the workers movement in particular opened up a wide field of successful entrepreneurial activities. They paved the way for new forms of business and exercised an educative influence. If, applying a severe yardstick, it is desired to find out how far cooperative societies themselves are really of a commonweal character, we must examine their merits case by case (31). Considering their history and their social intentions, the hypothesis that they are really of a commonweal character should surely be justified.

All cooperative societies, of course, want to champion their members' interests. In the case of producers' societies the aim is to maximize the nominal or money income of the members, while for consumers' societies serving households an increase of real income per household is sought (32). Differences in members' interests will always determine the pricing policy of cooperative societies. By these means purchasing cooperatives of artisans and traders can practise certain commonweal functions "provided that the members do not use the advantages obtained on their behalf by their cooperative merely for the purpose of increasing their standard of living, . . . but pass these advantages on to their customers through price reductions . . . in such a way as to bring about positive consequences for competition as well as an increase of demand from the increased real income of consumers" (33). A high cooperative dividend may have the same result.

In the case of selling cooperatives, especially those of the middle-classes, which generally do not supply final consumers, improvements of business structure are their first preoccupation. This, in principle, is also a commonweal aim. Whether and to what extent the solution of middle-class problems of business structure by means of cooperative societies runs counter to the interests of other social groups, depends on the policy of the middle-classes and upon agricultural policy, neither of which is decided by cooperative societies. It is always a success in itself if a cooperative enterprise, working on behalf of the economic interests of its members, simultaneously exercises educational functions by developing an attitude, more rational and more in conformity with market conditions, and contributes to the perfection of the market.

FREE COMMONWEAL ENTERPRISE

Joint business concerns of a commonweal character, which have been built up by the German Workers' Movement, are presently, along with consumers' cooperative societies, the most conspicuous form of free commonweal enterprise. Together with other forms of enterprise of a non-profit-making character, they constitute a diverse group competing with private enterprise.

In an economic system basically directed by the profit motive this type of free commonweal enterprise is intended to pursue a policy of structural reform and increased competition. This kind of enterprise mostly assumes the company form and does not limit its activities to its members. We may characterize it as follows: big organizations, e.g. trade unions, or big enterprises like the consumers' cooperative societies contribute the basic capital, prescribing objectives aimed at the common good. A management committee will ensure that these tasks are fulfilled (35).

During the last two decades, a considerable number of such commonweal enterprises have come into being in various fields, and they have conducted themselves well under competitive conditions in a free market. These concerns are no longer groups or firms of a particular class for a particular class, for they now foster objectives in the common interest.

This type of free commonweal enterprise has proved to be so efficient, that it is apt to replace other types of enterprise, which are no longer well adapted to modern conditions. The new type is appropriate not only for business units, which have up to now adopted the cooperative form, but also for many kinds of public enterprise, which in this form could better fulfil their basic mission.

Free commonweal enterprise can also help with macro-economic tasks. They may assist the government in its efforts to control economic forces, provided that neither their business autonomy nor their principle activities are impaired. In the formation of economic policy they can help bridge the gap between central power and the decentralized parts of the economy. Pursuing commonweal goals with determination, such firms may even induce private producers to undertake activities, which are in the common interest. Commonweal enterprise admits of the possibility of bringing about a synthesis of these two basic forces

This type of free commonweal enterprise is also quite appropriate for non-capitalist systems. The planned economies of the Eastern countries might find it helpful to introduce decentralized elements as a counterweight to their central direction. In the "Third World", the developing countries, this type of enterprise might even prove to be the most appropriate form of business. By means of commonweal enterprise, pre-industrial structures may be activated in such countries into entrepreneurial activities, wherever a class of private entrepreneurs is missing and/or whenever private enterprise is not desired. In such a way it might be possible to counteract an unbalanced growth of the state sector during development, and it might be possible to release in the population certain sources of energy, which would otherwise remain untapped (36).

With their help, the way may even be cleared for private enterprise, as soon as it is desired. It is widely recognized that a tremendous task rests on the cooperative movement in this sphere. The decisive part played by commonweal enterprises of "Histadrut" (the trade union organization) in the industrialization of Israel is also well-known.

Chapter 3

COMMONWEAL ENTERPRISE – STAGES IN THE DEVELOPMENT OF COOPERATIVES

The best-known and most active "free" commonweal enterprise in Germany today are the business units owned by trade unions and by the German consumers' societies. Their history may be divided into two periods. The first is that of cooperative enterprises in their two forms as producers' cooperatives and consumers' cooperatives. The second period is dominated by commonweal companies owned by trade union federations and consumers' cooperative associations, with the companies operating as free commonweal enterprises on the open market in the legal form of joint-stock company.

These types of enterprise in their chronological order represent non-profit oriented business units developed by anti-capitalist forces in the 19th century and the first decade of the 20th as an alternative to private enterprise. Free commonweal enterprise is the final form of these. It should be emphasized that the first fully effective and competitive modern free commonweal enterprises were developed by the German workers movement and by the consumers' cooperatives.

PRODUCERS' COOPERATIVE SOCIETIES

As has already been pointed out, the social movement, especially the workers' movement, began with experiments carried out by the early Socialists. Modern non-profit seeking enterprises had their origin in the "Utopias". Freedom as inaugurated by the French Revolution had brought in its wake industrialization and with it new capitalist enterprises, which broke up old structures, but led to a further loss of freedom for the masses. The loss of freedom in this period was even worse than in feudal times as it was the consequence of surplus population. This surplus gave rise to an industrial reserve army, for which no adequate living conditions existed at the time.

To the extent that the surplus population did not emigrate overseas, it settled around the new factories, and this explains why the new state of wretchedness was first attributed to the new capitalist ventures. It was quite understandable that people should want to counteract capitalist enterprise, which in their eyes was tantamount to misery and injustice, by setting up non-capitalist concerns to effect justice and an improved living standard.

The first foundations to occur now look rather fantastic. We must, however, remember that the protagonists of the social movement and of the nascent workers' movement could hardly hold other ideas in the circumstances. As Robert Michels wrote, the working-class was, in those days, particularly receptive to Utopian ideas aimed at a new state, a new economic system, a new mankind and a new morality, and were ready to re-create everything "ab ovo". They had not yet any ideals of their own, and the old guild or corporative traditions no longer counted. Moreover, the working-class of those days was of a rather motley composition, comprising artisans, smallholders, and rural and domestic workers (37). "The novelty of what had to be done corresponded logically to the novelty of the situation for these newcomers." (38) This explains why people were searching for the new man, and were emigrating to the New World, where they intended to create new conditions in socialist colonies.

The tendency towards absolute solutions and Utopian projects and the belief that systems, which were in themselves contradictory, could be realized, bore witness to the newness of the workers' movement. They suffered, too, from the naive belief that it would be possible to persuade entrepreneurs to join the movement simply by appealing to their sense of justice and reasonableness. It is said that Fournier stayed at home every day between midday and 1 p.m. waiting for the millionaire, who would offer him the money for the foundation of the first phalanstery. From 1848 onwards, however, it became increasingly clear that these gentlemen "could only be enlightened by a stroke of lightning" (39). It was only the revolution of 1848 which brought disillusionment and some sober-minded re-evaluation.

The discussion at this time was basically confined to producers' cooperatives, for it was the classical form of cooperative society for the socialists of the sixties.

The producers' society is very probably the oldest type of cooperative society. Max Weber points out that ore mines had been run by producers' societies in the early Middle Ages (40). The term "producers' society" means a cooperative, in which the members jointly produce certain articles, which are then sold on behalf of the society. In such an enterprise the workers are simultaneously the entrepreneurs.

A distinction must be made between genuine and pseudo-producers' societies. Genuine societies are those, in which every member is simultaneously a worker and every worker simultaneously a cooperator. Furthermore, in principle, all societies are open, which means that anyone, who wants to become a member is able to do so. On the other hand pseudo-producers' cooperatives are those that do not offer open membership. The same term may be applied to producers' societies, which have partners, and especially those, which employ workers, who are not members. Whenever such a deviation exists, the producers' society as an institution is weakened. In such a case the producers' society is transformed into a business company, because cooperators assume the function of business partners or share-holders.

REASONS FOR THE FAILURE OF PRODUCERS' SOCIETIES

Genuine producers' societies, in the strict sense of the word, existed only in statu nascendi (41), as historical development has proved. We may leave aside the situation in the Eastern countries, Russian kolchozes, Chinese communes and the particular forms of enterprise existing in Yugoslavia, as well as Mexican ejidos. These enterprises are, with the exception of the Mexican ejidos, mere organs of a planned economic system, i.e. state enterprises, which have the participation of workers, and which are more or less legitimized by the fact that they parade as producers' societies. Today, genuine and autonomous producers' societies competing with capitalist enterprises exist in practice only in the case of some religious sects, which are isloated from the outside world, and which are trying to be completely self-sufficient, or in the case of groups that adopt a defensive attitude in the face of a hostile environment. Among the producers' societies of the first type we may count the agricultural cooperatives of the Hutterites in North America (42) and in the other the Israeli kibbutz. In both cases, the breakdown or transformation of these producers' societies begins, as experience has shown, with a secularization of the cooperative idea, and this as a rule occurs, whenever the hostile environment subsides. There are other producers' societies, at least in name, in a variety of places, especially in France, where about six hundred of them still exist (43).

All of them, however, are so watered down as to be hardly recognizable. As Franz Oppenheimer has said, the history of producers' societies shows an uninterrupted sequence of failures (44), and it is simply not true, as is still frequently argued, that these societies failed because of a lack of capital (45).

As is well known, Lassalle considered that the shortage of capital was the real reason why producers' societies failed and he, therefore, asked Bismarck to grant state aid to producers' societies. Schulze-Delitzsch also believed that capital shortage was an impediment to the success of producers' societies, and he saw in his credit societies an instrument to permit workers and artisans to save the necessary capital to found producers' societies.

The capital shortage argument cannot be accepted, because the problem of how to obtain the necessary capital exists for any other enterprise in much the same way as for producers' societies. Many of the successful founders of capitalist enterprises have been penniless artisans or workers, who nevertheless developed vast enterprises. Successful producers' societies could even have obtained loans. "It is clear from a large number of producers' societies, which failed because of financial difficulties, that they had sufficient means to carry on their enterprise, and that they had no more difficulty with sales than the average entrepreneur" (46).

The capital shortage argument holds only in so far as there is no reason to believe that many large groups of workers would be ready to starve themselves in order to build up their society.

The lower income groups in any society always show a high propensity to consume, because the standard of living taken as a norm and observed by all concerned is always fixed by one of the higher income groups, so that the lower income groups exhibit no great savings potential (47). There will always be a small number of people ready to behave as ascetics, but we may not presume that entire classes of society will be prepared to behave in such a manner (48).

It might, of course, be possible to provide for a certain minimum of self-financing in the statutes of producers' societies. We must not forget, however, that, in a cooperative society a vote may be held on any issue at any time, and, therefore, there is the danger that self-financing will be sacrificed, sooner or later, to higher consumption or to the corresponding social benefits, and that this danger will be greater in a producers' society than in private enterprise. In a large-scale private undertaking large withdrawals on personal account often amount to only a small fraction of realized profits. Nevertheless, when we examine the reasons, why private enterprise, and even private business of medium size, fail, we always find that one of the reasons, and often not the least unimportant, lies in the fact that the entrepreneur withdrew funds at a rate, which was simply too high. This withdrawal of funds often takes place despite the entrepreneur's better judgement and better self and is to be explained by the fact that small and medium-size entrepreneurs live under the social constraint of "conspicuous consumption" to uphold their class-standard. If this fact leads to business failures in these circles, it is even more likely to apply to simple workers from lower income groups, to whom it is daily demonstrated how pleasant affluence is. The real problem, therefore, does not lie in the shortage of capital but in the realm of private living standards, and for that reason, grants from the state, as desired by Lassalle, can hardly ever be justified. Besides, the principle of state aid may not be generally applicable. Only the principle of self-help always remains relevant, and this principle has been followed successfully by consumers' societies, by Schulze-Delitzsch and by Raiffeisen.

OPPENHEIMERS' "LAW OF TRANSFORMATION"

The chief reason why producers' societies failed was a different one and has been called "the law of transformation" by Franz Oppenheimer (49). This law states that producers' societies must transform themselves into joint-stock companies, if they do not want to go under. The fact that their membership is not closed and that every cooperator is a worker means that they are not able to survive in a free market economy. Because of these two principles the interests of the cooperative as a whole and of the individual do not coincide. When there is a rise in demand, it is in the interests of the producers' society to recruit new members, but this is not so for the original members, who have then to share the profits over a larger number of heads without any assurance that the boom will last. When demand falls, the interest of the society calls for a limitation to production. Individual members, however, in such a situation are concerned to increase production because they want a continued high income for themselves and their families. Furthermore, the interests of the cooperative society and of its members clash in the case of capital formation. To solve all these questions according to democratic rules is beyond the intellectual ability of the members.

Oppenheimer points out that fundamental differences exist between sellers' and buyers' cooperatives. In the sellers' society, to which group the producers' society belongs, the inherent conflict between individual and group interest is encountered. For this reason, the sellers' society can not exist without some constraints. The situation is different, however, in the case of buyers' societies, to which consumers' societies belong. In this case, the interests of both coincide. Buyers' societies may, therefore, behave in conformity with the rules of the market.

For instance, whenever the price of a product purchased by a buyer rises, both, buyers and society, will diminish their demand. In the case of price reductions both will also act in complete conformity. For buyers' societies the principle of the open door is not a problem. When the buyers' society is successful, new members can join in, and the bigger the society is, the more successfully it can work on behalf of its members.

In a study of the British cooperative movement Beatrice Webb, who published under her maiden name of Potter, maintained that a producers' society managed by the workers themselves would be neither socialist nor democratic but "individualistic" (50).

The constitution of the producers' society represents a contradiction in itself. According to the cooperative constitution, equality and complete democracy should prevail. When, however, the society reaches a certain size, a differentiation of function becomes necessary, e.g. a greater executive independence has to be accorded to the management. Now, it is obvious that the producers' society will not be able to grant such independence, unless it transforms itself into an ordinary business unit. The producers' society will, therefore, prove incapable of taking over methods of modern large-scale production. This is the reason, why it is bound to fail. It does not represent progress, but is backward-looking, for it harps back to pre-industrial forms of production.

There is only one surprising aspect of the producers' society, and that is the fact that such a vast amount of thinking has been devoted to this rather impracticable form of enterprise, and that so many long-lived experiments have been carried out with them. I would presume that the real reason for this is that in the past such attempts were based upon faulty economic reasoning. In the second half of the 19th century, economists were fascinated by the idea of a stationary economy.

In a stationary economy there would be no entrepreneurial profits and no interest. Both result from growth and development (51). In a stationary economic system all income would belong to the two original factors of production, labour and land. Capital would not have any value, because, depreciation apart, it would not be in demand. In a static economic system the profits of entrepreneurs and interest on capital would simply represent wages which have not been paid out, and, therefore, exploitation. In such an economic system the producers' society would be an ideal and effective form of enterprise. As these conditions are not met, producers' societies working without internal or external constraint cannot exist, as they could not compete with private enterprise.

The other reasons, which are often quoted for the failure of producers' societies, viz. the shortage of entrepreneurial personality (52), and the lack of discipline among the staff can also be traced back to a false theoretical basis (53). Even a capable personality in the position of a manager may be able to do little, if the post does not carry the necessary powers. The later history of the German consumers' society and of other commonweal enterprises has shown that the German workers' movement has at its disposal a great number of people able to fulfil entrepreneurial functions. An enterprise of an unworkable structure may not thrive even with the most capable entrepreneur at its helm.

As has been pointed out by W. Engelhardt the producers' society has, nevertheless, retained a certain importance in spite of its failure (54). It was the consistent expression of a new idea of an economic system and the most explicit form of an ideal, viz. of a cooperative system based on the consent of all participants.

THE CONSUMERS' COOPERATIVE SOCIETIES

The consumers' cooperatives compared with producers'

cooperatives proved to be workable forms of enterprise. In a consumers' society, there is no clash between the needs of individual members and the needs of the society as a whole. Consumers' societies also benefit from the principle of the open door. The profits, furthermore, are not distributed per head, but by means of a cooperative dividend based upon the purchases effected by the number. This encourages the members of the society to increase their purchases. All this constitutes a complex of factors, which furthers the success of the society in contrast to the experience of producers' cooperatives.

W. M. Kirsch has designated the principle of the cooperative dividend as the third way to distribute profits (55). In the capitalist way, profits are handed over to owners of capital, while in the socialist method, in producers' cooperative societies, the profits go to the workers. Through the principle of cooperative dividends the consumers receive the surplus. This seems to be a well-justified manner of distribution, being at the same time successful and businesslike, as has been proved by the history of consumers' societies. In the following chapters they will be considered in greater detail.

Chapter 4

COMMONWEAL JOINT STOCK AND LIMITED LIABILITY COMPANIES

The consumers' cooperative society, as a form of enterprise, is appropriate only for the joint purchase of goods and services. In practice, it remains limited to the realm of retail trade. In spite of its successes there was still a need to have other forms of enterprise, which were not profit-oriented and which would also be workable outside the retail trade. This requirement was met by enterprises in the form of associations, ordinary trade partnerships or, in most cases, by joint stock companies, which began operating in Germany from the second half of the last century onwards as businesses of either the central associations of consumers' societies or of individual consumers' societies.

INDUSTRIAL ACTIVITIES OF CONSUMERS' SOCIETIES

As with the idea of producers' societies, the idea of production carried on specifically for the requirements of the working class could not be successfully realized, despite the fact that the idea had been current for at least one generation. It is easy to explain this from the point of view of industrial economics. For a large commercial firm – the original aim of consumers' societies in their new ventures – it will always be more advantageous to buy its goods from the cheapest producer, wherever that is, instead of only selling goods produced by its own industrial establishments. A large commercial enterprise disposes of great purchasing power. It promises greater success to bring this power to bear rather then build its own industrial establishments to supply its own goods (56).

To be successful, the producer must have a firm grip on the suppliers if he requires special qualities and particular kinds of goods, for otherwise he may have to expect discrimination to be exercised by his suppliers.

In the retail trade it is in most cases not advisable to take over one's suppliers. If one does, one is simply tying up capital without being sure that these establishments will be able to produce enough at favourable prices. Today, there is one further argument against such industrial establishments. In modern self-service shops there is no longer any sales talk; the buyer takes automatically the best-known brands, which are supported by efficient advertising campaigns. Producers' brands, the sales and production of which remain relatively limited, can hardly ever spend as much on advertising as firms whose brands are available everywhere; nor is it possible to offer exclusively one's own products in a modern self-service shop. The buyer wants to see a complete selection of all brands, even where 90% of the turn-over comes from only two of ten brands. Retail firms' own brands are, therefore, only practicable in areas, where the market is not yet dominated by well-advertised brands. This is true of bakeries, butcher-shops and wine-cellars of the consumers' societies.

ESTABLISHMENTS OF THE TRADE UNIONS

Parallel to the consumers' societies the Trade Unions also began, around the turn of the century, to build up their own establishments to meet certain needs of their members (57). They founded mostly insurance companies, hotels, and building and housing societies. Almost all trade unions and civil servants associations founded such firms shortly after the First World War.

The task of catering specially for the members of a particular association limits, as a rule, the development of the firm concerned. It creates an artificial narrowness to the market and, therefore, represents an inefficient form of specialization.

Limiting the undertaking to production for a particular group of people is only economically sensible, if this group forms its own special market, as is the case with a number of professions or hobbies, and where there is a clearly defined and special demand for particular clothing, instruments or food. The detailed knowledge of the producer or dealer then compensates for the narrowness of the market.

Things are different when the specialization is governed by extra-economic considerations, no matter whether the criteria are of a political, social, religious or racial character. Entrepreneurs specializing in particular fields determined by extra-economic considerations, renounce, voluntarily, certain sales possibilities. Preference accorded to certain customers implies, at the same time, neglect of others. Above all, the particular group at which the producer or trader is aiming, generally expects that it will be able to purchase its goods at lower prices than elsewhere. Any voluntary limitation of this kind contradicts the "law of mass production" and, therefore, the principle of business efficiency, so that each producer or trader behaving in this way will not be able to compete with normal traders or producers in the long run. The reason, why such firms fail is that the task they set themselves does not accord with sound business principles.

There have been many attempts to found banking establishments by trade unions. The idea of investing liquid trade union funds in their own banks is as old as the German Trade Unions themselves. Civil servants' associations have been particularly eager to found such establishments. They tried to build up their own civil servants' banks under cooperative guise. They were intended to form a third cooperative credit branch alongside the People's Banks and the Raiffeisen Banks.

The idea that such a limited bank could be useful contradicts the basic principle of banking. The founders of such institutes overlooked the fact that a bank is based upon one very simple principle, viz. that it lends out its depositors' money to other people, in an attempt at optimum diversification. A bank should accept deposits from as many people as possible, with as diversified payment habits and cash needs as possible, and lend the money to as many borrowers as possible with as different maturity dates as possible. A bank which is limited to a particular group does not enjoy such diversification. It can, therefore, never be much more than a cashier's department parading as a bank. Such an establishment will be under the permanent threat of a lack of ready funds and is, therefore, obliged to hold a greater amount of cash than other banks. This will again diminish profits, and consequently such a credit institution cannot offer really favourable terms to trade unions and their members for their deposits and loans. The same argument applies to insurance companies, whose risks will be better the more diverse their customers.

COMMONWEAL ENTERPRISE

In the long run there was only one type of enterprise in all those founded by the workers' movement which proved really workable, the so-called "free commonweal enterprise". The first enterprise of the German workers' movement, which adopted the form of a joint stock company, was the insurance company "Volksfürsorge", which was owned jointly by trade unions and cooperatives (58). The idea of founding such an enterprise was originally formulated by the President of the "Kaiserliches Aufsichtsamt für das Versicherungswesen" (Imperial Control Office for Insurance Companies), who thought that a commonweal enterprise was necessary to overcome the catastrophic conditions prevailing at the time in small-scale life insurance. He asked the private insurance companies shortly before the First World War to create an insurance company catering for small-scale life insurance, and which would not be based upon pure profit principles. Such an enterprise was intended to eliminate all sorts of abuses, offering small-scale insurance policies on reasonable conditions. As the private insurance companies refused to comply, the trade unions and consumers' societies jointly founded the insurance company "Volksfürsorge" (59).

Even today the "Volksfürsorge" remains an almost pure-to-type free commonweal enterprise. It is comparatively easy to describe this type of free commonweal enterprise. Large associations which are more than simple pressure groups, for instance trade unions or consumers' societies, supply the necessary capital for such an enterprise and in so doing renounce high profits. The legal form of such an enterprise is usually that of a joint stock company or even a limited liability company. The board of directors will be nominated by share-holders. But it also contains presidents of trade unions or members of executive committees of consumers' societies. By their participation they guarantee the commonweal character of such a firm. It is, therefore, not absolutely necessary that commonweal aims should be explicitly mentioned in the statutes or elsewhere.

This type of enterprise has proved its viability in the free market. This may be seen from the fact that in the last fifteen years a considerable complex of such commonweal enterprises have made their appearance, in a number of quite different fields. These commonweal enterprises do not cater exclusively for trade union members or members of consumers' cooperatives, as is frequently asserted. They are not enterprises founded by members of associations and catering exclusively for them, but they put their goods and services at everyone's disposal. Commonweal enterprises of this kind serve consumers in general, pursuing by entrepreneurial means aims that are in the general interest. They are no longer concerns of a particular group working for a particular group but they are enterprises following aims of a general economic kind. In comparison to all previous types of enterprises of the workers' movement, they represent something fundamentally new.

COMPARISON OF FOUR DEVELOPMENT STAGES

From this survey of the history of non profit-oriented enterprises of the German workers' movement we may draw two conclusions: first of all, there will be a tendency for commonweal and commercial enterprises to converge in certain areas and to diverge increasingly in other areas.

1. The legal and organizational forms of the four types of enterprises with which we are dealing, have adapted in the course of their development more and more to the form of private enterprise.

2. On the other hand the behaviour of these concerns, which are not pursuing profits, has adapted more and more to commonweal principles. Producers' societies in their internal structure were organized as the antithesis to profit-oriented businesses, basing themselves upon the principle of direct democracy. There was neither division of power between the executive and the owners, nor full-time management composed of experts. The consumers' societies, however, soon developed full-time management and their own organs for supervisory and auditing purposes. Finally the establishments owned by central organizations of the consumers' societies and by trade unions assumed not only capitalist legal business forms, but also capitalist forms of organization.

Commonweal enterprises have followed the principle of division of power to its conclusion. The owners, i.e. the executive committees of trade unions and of consumers' societies nominate the members of the board of directors. The management is composed of experts. Now, it is logical that the only thing expected from the experts is that they remain loyal towards the aim of the enterprise concerned; but they are no longer required to identify themselves politically or socially with them. Staff moves between commonweal enterprises and private firms just as it moves among private firms in the same field. Commonweal enterprises in general have tended to adapt themselves in formal aspects to those of private enterprise.

Things are different, when it comes to the aims and performance. The objectives pursued by commonweal enterprise and by private enterprise are in ever greater conflict. On the market, the producers' societies have behaved like purely private firms. Their founders envisaged that in the distant future, producers' societies would be able to exchange goods among themselves according to the labour theory of value, because they thought that the entire economic system would then have been transformed into producers' societies. Until then, the producers' societies should fulfil their commonweal aims by re-distributing the profits of the enterprise in a different way. Profit would no longer flow into the pockets of capitalists but be distributed to the workers. In such a way, a privileged group of workers would replace capital owners, who had hitherto been the privileged. It is true, that the surplus of the producers' societies is also used for private purposes, but the distribution of profits is carried out in a more socialist manner.

On the other hand consumers' societies represent a change in behaviour. They pay out surpluses by means of the cooperative dividend, according to the purchases of each member. Because anybody can join a consumers' society, it represents a form of enterprise in which a minority no longer appropriates the profits at the expense of the community at large (60).

Commonweal enterprises go one step further yet. Producers' or consumers' societies only return profits obtained on the market to the workers or member, but free commonweal enterprises operate actively on the market, using their profits for such purposes as correspond to the higher interests of the community. The principles of behaviour of the non-profit motivated enterprises developed in two main ways, as they changed from producers' societies through consumers' societies and association undertakings to commonweal enterprises. First, there is the transition from the principle of profit-sharing among the workers of producers' cooperatives to the principle of the dividend to members of the consumers' cooperative and, secondly, the transition from the principle of the dividend to the new market behaviour of the commonweal enterprise.

This new market behaviour of commonweal enterprises may be called the principle of the use of profits through business activity on behalf of the community and society in general.

Parallel to this modification in behaviour and in the use of profits, there is also a change in the aims pursued and the adversary, against whom the operations are carried out. The old friend and enemy relationship is abolished, and new coalitions are formed. The producers' society always saw itself in opposition to private capitalist business, especially in industry. Consumers' societies had only one adversary left, viz. middle-class retail enterprise. In contrast to the hostility prevailing between capitalist entrepreneurs and producers' societies, consumers' societies and private retailers no longer deny each other the right to exist.

As a general rule, however, commonweal enterprise no longer has any specific adversary; there is no class and no group, which they want to eliminate. Their aim is no longer to remain as a lone victor on the battle-field after a market struggle. They fight only abuses and abnormal conditions and are complementary to the private economy, wherever it does not function. In this case they are ready to enter coalitions of a changing character with private groups of entrepreneurs. They also try to give positive examples and to act as models.

Such a convergence of form, accompanied by divergence in real actions, signifies that there will be a considerable increase in commonweal activities by non-commercial enterprise. The producers' societies remained passive in their market conduct; they only paid out profits earned on the market. Things were different in the case of the consumers' societies: by varying the amount of cooperative dividends, they exercised an influence on surrounding markets in the interest of all consumers. Consumers' societies were already using the cooperative form of profit distribution to pursue commonweal aims.

In the case of commonweal enterprise the use of profits by the enterprise in the interest of the community and for the common good is the dominant aim. They are no longer primarily an instrument of a policy of re-distribution. Their tasks, therefore, do not consist in a redistribution of the social product in a way different from profit-oriented production.

They are, on the contrary, an autonomous instrument for a policy of fostering competition and structural change with the mission of correcting, regulating and providing examples to make and maintain the efficacy of markets.

Chapter 5

THE FOUR PILLARS OF THE WORKERS' MOVEMENT

In the second half of last century the miserable economic condition of the German working class and of many artisans was the reason for practical activities at all levels of life to improve, in stages, the position of the worker in the whole of his field of interest. These activities took place independently of all philosophical, economic and political discussions. To help an oppressed group of people it is not enough to increase their wages. A whole array of measures must be applied; professional qualifications have to be improved, prestige and public recognition must be increased to liberate energies so far frustrated. Resignation, resentment and all forms of inferiority complex must be swept away. Simultaneously, the need for information and communication and the desire to gain some social influence increase in these groups. Such needs also have to be catered for. When people talk only of wages to emancipate oppressed groups instead of considering these sociological and psychological factors, this is because the factors mentioned above assume the character of a symbol, and the so-called "universe of workers' interests" in the day to day political struggle, has been translated into the language of a fight between economic interests.

The struggle for economic and social integration assumed distinctive forms of organization at an early date. The organizations of the workers' movement tried to solve this problem essentially by four different means: *1*. Through influence on the legislator; *2*. through influence on the employer; *3*. through raising the intellectual and cultural level of the working-class, and *4*. through measures of mutual aid. In such a way the "four pillars" of the workers' movement developed in the course of time: the workers' parties, the trade unions, the cultural organizations and the industrial and commercial establishments of the workers' movement. The stability and dynamics of the German workers' movement were largely based upon the fact that it had a very extensive range of organizations and enterprises, so that every single worker could be taken care of, literally, from the cradle to the grave.

This extensive structure of organizations comprising the whole "universe of workers' interests" gave the necessary self-respect to the worker, who had so far been an outcast. The structure also brought about the possibility, at the organizational level, of developing the necessary solidarity in the struggle for liberation and of creating, at the same time, hopes for the future. These hopes developed and extended, giving the working class the strength necessary to enable it, step by step, to improve its situation. This was done by means of numerous reform measures, each one the result of a tough struggle. In this way the working-class escaped from its undeserved misery, and the workers were transformed into citizens enjoying more or less equal rights. This occurred despite heavy reverses from time to time. No single "pillar" could have reached this point alone.

The success of the political parties, aiming at the improvement of the working class position, is well-known and no description of their development is given here. They brought about many reforms, either directly or indirectly helped by trade unions, for instance the social insurance scheme and the compulsory sickness insurance, the eight-hour working day, a law on working conditions and the institution of shop stewards. In the Federal Republic, measures regarding workers' control were introduced, and old-age pensions were made "dynamic", i.e. they were tied to the wage level. The trade unions, the second "pillar" of the workers' movement, fought slowly and against heavy odds, for freely negotiated wage contracts, defined hours of work, and the equalization of the conditions of workers and employees. They also developed the form of wage determination which is current today.

The third pillar, the cultural organizations of the workers' movement, is no longer important. It has been more or less absorbed into the local, public and non-party cultural and sporting organizations, to which it has transmitted many impulses. Workers' and community interests more or less coincide in this area. In many institutions, their origin in the workers' movement can only be recognized from their names, as when the term "people" occurs in the name. We may quote as examples the "People's High School" (Evening Institute) and the "People's Theatre".

In the twenties the workers' sports organizations had been very strong, but they have disappeared into non-party organizations.

The fourth pillar consisted of consumers' societies and of establishments belonging to the workers' movement. On the basis of this fourth pillar, the "free" commonweal enterprises developed as we see them today, especially the group of the cooperative societies, the insurance company "Volksfürsorge", the public-utility building society "Neue Heimat" (New Home), and the "Bank für Gemeinwirtschaft" (Commonweal Bank).

TEMPORARY DIFFERENCES AMONG THE PILLARS OF THE WORKERS' MOVEMENT

The cooperative societies and the individual pillars of the workers' movement developed successively, established contact only gradually, and recognized each other only after some time. There have been, moreover, many divergencies of opinion among them. The German Social-Democratic Party was the youngest of the four pillars from a historical point of view, and at first it refused to recognize the older organizations, viz. the trade unions and also the consumers' cooperative society, which still represented commonweal enterprise to a very large extent in those days. There had already been a wave of founding consumers' cooperatives at the end of the eighteen-fifties, and in many cases consumers' cooperatives accepted only workers as members. The consumers' cooperatives were founded by workers' cultural associations, which had also sprung up at this time. These cooperatives still remained of a somewhat marginal character. Nevertheless, these pioneer actions together with the successes of consumers' cooperatives of the British workers' movement should have been an indication that here had been founded an adequate form of self-help for trade unionists.

In Germany the Marxists were always very reserved towards the cooperative societies, while they absolutely opposed the early socialists' experiments. The Marxists at this time thought that the consumers' cooperative society, as a form of enterprise, would be incapable of concentration, and that cooperative societies would never get beyond dwarf-like enterprises.

For this reason they thought consumers' cooperatives could never make a contribution towards the transformation of capitalist society. Marxists even dissuaded the workers from getting into contact with consumers' cooperatives. They thought that consumers' cooperatives only scratched the surface of the economic essence of capitalism, and that they could not attack the basic foundation of capitalism. The theoreticians of Marxism only recognized producers' cooperatives as a socially relevant form of enterprise, and one which they considered to be an important social experiment. Even in this case, however, they were convinced that this form of enterprise could only show what was in any case well-known to them, viz. that the existing system of capitalist order should be transformed and be replaced by a republican system of free and equal producers which would increase living standards. "For all Socialists of the sixties the producers' cooperative was the real cooperative, but they accepted the consumers' cooperative into the bargain" (61).

THE OPINION OF KARL MARX ON "WORKERS COOPERATIVE FACTORIES"

It must be emphasized that Karl Marx had not yet arrived at a fundamental critique of cooperation (62). He had said only a few, though positive, words, in the third volume of *Das Kapital* about the "workers cooperative factories", as he called the producers' cooperatives. He saw in them alternatives to capitalist enterprises. "The workers' cooperative factories . . . are the first breakthrough within the old structure, though naturally enough they reproduce and must reproduce the failings of the present system in their organization. Nevertheless, the conflict between capital and labour has been eliminated in these enterprises, if only by the fact that workers by association are their own capitalists, i.e. they use the means of production to realize their own labour. They show how at a certain level of development of the material productive forces and of the corresponding social forms of production, a new means of production develops and expands on the basis of the former" (63).

As Bernstein said, Marx arrived at this judgement on producers' cooperatives primarily by deductive methods, because this form of a cooperative society corresponded to his dialectics and represented, according to his social theory, a direct opposite to capitalist enterprise (64). The producers' society as a dialectic counterweight "also corresponds apparently to the notion of the fundamental contradiction in modern production, and one in need of urgent solution, between already socialized labour and the still private appropriation of production. The producers' cooperative appears as a practical solution to this contradiction within the framework of individual enterprises. In this sense Marx considers that . . . the contradiction between capital and labour has therefore been eliminated in a positive way, and that it has shown that the capitalist entrepreneur is really superfluous" (65).

LASSALLE'S OPPOSITION TO CONSUMERS' COOPERATIVE SOCIETIES

Lassalle was absolutely opposed to consumers' cooperative societies, not on grounds of experience, but as a result of "the iron law of wages", which he expounded. His attitude found its clearest expression in the "Offenes Antwortschreiben" (Open Reply), a programme pamphlet submitted in 1863 to the Constituent Assembly of the "Allgemeiner Deutscher Arbeiterverein" (General German Workers' Association), the first comprehensive social-democratic organization. The question of how to find a socialist form of enterprise was in the centre of social and political discussion of those days, as may be seen from the fact that this pamphlet examines to a very large extent, the problem of the producers' cooperative society.

In this pamphlet, Lassalle expounds the theory that the consumers' cooperative societies are completely incapable of bringing about an improvement of the situation of the working-class (66). He asserted that the activities of consumers' cooperatives would be thwarted by the "iron law of wages", since the average wage would always remain reduced to the subsistence level, which was the amount required, through custom, for existence and procreation. The wage rate could never rise above this average in the long run, for any slight improvement in the situation of workers would bring about an increase in the population and, therefore, an increase in "hands" offered, which would depress the wage to its former level (67).

From this it follows that consumers' cooperatives cannot help the workers: "As long as only limited groups of workers join consumers' cooperatives, average wages will not be touched by the activity, and consumers' cooperatives will offer their working-class members some minor relief to their depressed condition through the cheaper prices of commodities. However, as soon as consumers' cooperatives include more and more of the entire working-class population, the economic law we have quoted will lead to the inevitable consequence that wages must fall by the same amount as the consumers' cooperatives have reduced the expenses of consumption" (68). "Under the influence of this theory, the idea of consumers' cooperatives could only slowly gain a foot-hold in the German working-class" (69).

LASSALLE'S RECOMMENDATION OF PRODUCERS' SOCIETIES

Lassalle declared that only the producers' society could help workers in the long run. "To make the workers their own entrepreneurs – that is the means (and the only means) by which this cruel iron law, which determines the workers' wages can be eliminated"! "When the working-class is its own entrepreneur, the distinction between workers' wages and entrepreneurs' profit will be eliminated, and with it will completely disappear the crude wage, to be replaced as the remuneration of labour by the whole product of labour!" "The elimination of entrepreneurs' profits, in the most peaceful, legal and simplest way, viz. by organizing the working-class in voluntary associations as its own entrepreneur, is the only improvement of the situation of the working-class, which is not an illusion" (70). It should be the task of the State (according to Lassalle), to help the working-class through grants and credits, for it is the State's responsibility to further cultural progress. Small producers' cooperatives would not be able to get away from the domineering influence of the capitalist system, it they were limited solely to mutual aid. If they could not escape this influence, only the person of the entrepreneur would change, but this would not be of any help to the worker.

These two declarations, in favour of producers' cooperatives and against the consumers' cooperatives, which had been derived from theoretical premises, impeded for many years the development of consumers' cooperative societies. The producers' cooperatives which had been recommended were spectacularly unsuccessful, and workers were dissuaded from joining the successful consumers' cooperatives.

As a consequence the German Social-Democratic Party, in the first decades of its existence, declared itself officially against any entrepreneurial activity in the case of the trade unions as well as consumers' cooperatives. The Congress of the Social-Democratic Party in Berlin in 1892 even felt obliged to oppose the belief that consumers' cooperatives were in a position to influence the conditions of production under capitalism in order to improve the situation of the working-class, or to resolve or even alleviate the political and trade union class-struggle on behalf of the workers. August Bebel made similar pronouncements at a Congress of the party in Cologne (71). A trade union mass movement could, therefore, only begin in Germany at the end of the last century, and an independent movement of consumers' cooperatives within the framework of the workers' movement only began, under the influence of German "revisionism", after the turn of the century.

THE NEW ATTITUDE OF REVISIONISM

German Marxist revisionism, especially through its chief representative, Eduard Bernstein, contested the crisis theory of Marx, and instead demonstrated the possibility of an evolutionary development of modern capitalism, in the process of which the trade unions and the cooperative organizations had an important part to play. When revisionism asserted itself inside the workers' movement, the workers began to be interested in consumers' cooperatives, and the cooperatives were able to gain a foothold in the working-class. Under the influence of revisionism organized workers got away from the idea that they could only realize their aims by political methods. They were now ready to find a solution within the prevailing conditions and to examine also the small steps which could improve their position. From then on the workers began to found consumers' cooperatives in working-class areas, and then it was possible for the consumers' cooperatives to develop into a large, mass movement.

Nevertheless, some of the Socialist theoreticians remained hostile to the enterprises of the working-class or ignored them as a "quantité négligable". Consequently, there was the interesting phenomenon of the working-class over a period of years founding consumers'cooperatives against the will of its theoreticans, yet never was a movement more influenced by its great theoreticans than the German workers' movement during the nineteenth century. The fact that the working-class joined the consumers' cooperatives, independent of and for decades in opposition to the theoretical debates, may be considered a sort of minor revolt by the members against their own ideologists. They continued to listen with enthusiasm to scientific debates, while tackling at the same time, by practical means, topical questions at the local level in a manner in conflict with ruling doctrine. Acting in this way the small local organizations of the workers' movement did what was necessary for their daily requirements and, at the same time, what was theoretically correct. They had realized that their theoreticians were on quite the wrong track, though they did not know why, and they did the right thing, without knowing exactly what they were doing.

To my knowledge, only Eduard Bernstein saw things correctly in those days.

In his chief work *Die Voraussetzungen des Sozialismus und die Aufgaben der Sozialdemokratie (The Conditions of Socialism and the Tasks of Social-Democracy)*, Eduard Bernstein, in examining the question of working-class enterprise, dedicated a whole section to this problem in the fourth chapter under the title "Die Leistungsfähigkeit der Wirtschaftsgenossenschaften" ("The Efficacy of Economic Cooperatives"). He says there: "The cooperative society offers the opportunity to industrial workers of counteracting exploitation of commerce on the one hand, while on the other mobilizing means to make things easier for the whole liberation movement in various respects" (72). He asserted that the practical activities of Social-Democracy would lead to "the creation of circumstances and conditions allowing and consolidating a transformation of the modern order of society into a higher form without any convulsive accidents" (73). The liberal institutions of modern society were distinguished from those of the past by the very fact that they were capable of development. "They need not be ruptured, they must only be developed" (74). Organization, action and energy would be required for the purpose, but not necessarily revolutionary dictatorship. Bernstein, therefore, asks for increasing self-responsibility, and, from this point of view, he emphasizes the political value to the State, of trade unions, local and communal self-govenment and cooperative societies. From here on dates the recognition of cooperative societies and other enterprises of the fourth pillar of the workers' movement.

ALLIANCE BETWEEN CONSUMERS' COOPERATIVES AND TRADE UNIONS

In contrast with the Social-Democratic Party the members of the German trade unions recognized quite early the importance of consumers' cooperatives and realized that both movements were pursuing the same final aim.

At this time it was said that the aim of the trade union movement was the socialization and the democratization of production, whereas the cooperative movement aimed at the socialization and the democratization of consumption. Both movements were, therefore, complementary to each other. The struggle of the workers organized in trade unions to bring about an improvement of their living conditions, Bernstein wrote, was, as far as the capitalist was concerned, a struggle of the wage rate against the rate of profit. What the trade unions mean for the rate of profit in production, the consumers' cooperatives mean for the rate of profit in trading (75). The amicable relationship between the members of the free trade-unions and the members of the consumers' cooperative societies only led to cooperation at a higher level by both associations after the cooperative congress at Munich in 1910, and the trade-union congress at Dresden in 1911. In their congresses both organizations unanimously affirmed the aims of the consumers' cooperatives. Both desired that the economic power of the consumers' cooperatives be aimed at improving the standards of consumption, and be used in the service of social progress.

At these two congresses, agreement was also reached in areas where both organizations still occasionally quarrelled. The consumers' cooperatives declared that they would no longer sell any goods produced by sweated labour or in prisons. There was also agreement about the working conditions of employees in consumers' cooperatives and in its various factories. The consumers' cooperative concluded a collective agreement with the trade unions for their employees, an action which in the period before the First World War was nothing if not revolutionary.

ADOLF VON ELM, A PRACTICAL-MINDED MAN

A period of close collaboration between consumers' cooperatives and trade unions followed, and this was chiefly the result of the activities of some practical-minded men.

In this context, the activities of Adolf von Elm (1857–1916) are of great importance. We shall, therefore, describe them briefly (76). Adolf von Elm was the founder of the Association of cigar workers, from which he made a union. In 1891, after a four year period abroad in the era of the so-called "Law against Socialists", he founded a producers' cooperative of tobacco workers, after a strike had failed. Although there were some initial successes, he later recognized the weakness of this type of enterprise and linked it with the consumers' cooperatives. The cigar factory of the German consumers' cooperative movement, which still exists, may be traced back to the producers' cooperative of cigar workers founded by von Elm.

Von Elm participated actively in the foundation of the General Commission of the trade unions. In 1899, after a dock-workers' strike had failed, he founded the Consumers', Buildings' and Savings' Association "Produktion", which was the forerunner of the actual consumers' cooperative "Produktion", which still exists in Hamburg. If this consumers' cooperative developed rapidly, this may chiefly be attributed to the excellent statutes of this society, which had been decisively influenced by von Elm. In 1903 he actively participated in the foundation of the Central Association of German Consumers' Cooperative Societies. His last great work was the foundation of the insurance company "Volksfürsorge", which was founded jointly by the trade unions and the consumers' cooperatives and, until his death in 1916, he ran this enterprise as its first manager. For this reason Adolf von Elm is the creator of the modern type of commonweal enterprise and also the founder of the first enterprise of this type within the framework of the German consumers' cooperative movement and workers' movement. For many years, moreover, von Elm represented the Social-Democratic Party in the "Reichstag".

Adolf von Elm was a revisionist, in the sense of Bernstein. He declared that the working-class like the bourgeoisie and any other previous ruling class, would have to develop into a decisive force within society, before it could play this rôle in the state. He asserted that the working-class would in fact be able to exercise such an influence but it would first be necessary for them to organize themselves, not only to exercise influence on the state, but also on society.

With regard to the changing importance of the four "pillars", it is noteworthy that Elm attached a greater significance to the trade unions than the Social Democratic Party. He saw the real centre of power of the workers' movement in the trade unions, which required the political movement merely to complete their activities. The workers would obtain their freedom above all by their economic activities. The trade unions would, therefore, find an appropriate partner in the consumers' cooperatives. If both were supported with equal energy, persistence and solidarity by the workers, they would soon be in a position to alter significantly in their favour, the balance of power in society. The legislature, too, would then soon take account of this fact.

FRITZ NAPHTALI

At the turn of the century Adolf von Elm was the leading protagonist in the trade union and cooperative field. The next important figure in this area was a theoretical writer, the economist Fritz Naphtali (1888–1961) (77). He can be regarded as the leading theoretician of the "free" trade unions, of the Social Democratic Party and of public sector economics during these years. In his main work *Economic Democracy* he advocated the theory that the trade union and cooperative mutual-aid organizations along with public enterprises should aim to make the economy more democratic. This was the necessary rounding-off and completion of the recently won political democracy (78). Naphtali paid particular attention to public enterprise (79). In the cases of immediate mass needs, its particular importance would lie in those areas from which, by their very nature, competition was excluded in the long run. This field must then be denied to the private profit-regulated monopoly, as it was called in current terminology. In this context Naphtali was thinking mainly of transport business and insurance organizations. In these important sectors they would have to offer fair prices and also undertake the task of creating exemplary conditions of work for their employees, becoming thereby pacemakers in social policy.

The task of the consumers' cooperative movement would consist in forming countervailing power in the field of distribution to the benefit of buyers. This power could counter the "organized monopoly power" of industry, to use the terminology of the time (80). In businesses run by trade unions Naphtali saw a counterweight to a collective economy in the democratic sense, "for they represent a way, which could perhaps be more strongly developed in the future, for labour to penetrate into direct control of the economy, and thereby a method for democratizing the economy" (81).

The goal of increased democracy meant for Naphtali the complete permeation of the economy by the public interest, even as far as a communal evolution of property, in which the individual power of disposal would have no real meaning. In commonweal enterprises he saw an equally valid alternative form of organization to the state. This was essentially that "the control over the means of production through private property ownership for private ends should no longer belong to individuals but to the economic general interest incorporating the economic general will, in which public needs, rather than the private wants of individuals, should be the determining factor" (82).

It is an historical accident that the largest "free" commonweal undertakings in Federal Germany today are developments of consumers' cooperatives and are run by the consumers' cooperatives and trade unions. This circumstance arose from the fact that in the period of reconstruction in the aftermath of the Second World War the consumers' cooperatives and trade unions had the field to themselves, apart from government bodies, particularly the local authorities, which did not pursue purely profit motives. They alone let their undertakings pursue commonweal goals and presented them with new commonweal tasks predominantly in the field of structural and competition policy. In this way, the name "public economy" was fashioned for the enterprises of regional authorities and "Prafiski", for the concept of commonweal economy, was still employed only for the undertakings of consumers' cooperatives and trade unions. Therefore, one thinks today mainly of consumers' cooperatives, of the "Volksfürsorge", of the "Neue Heimat" and of the "Bank für Gemeinwirtschaft", when the discussion is of commonweal economy.

PART II

Commonweal Enterprise

Chapter 6

HISTORY OF THE GERMAN CONSUMERS' COOPERATIVES

From the congresses of 1910 and 1911 onwards we may consider the consumers' cooperatives as the fourth pillar of the workers' movement. Since that time, they have been serving the workers' universal interests in consumer affairs.

The founders of the British consumers' cooperative movement, the weavers of Rochdale, were workers in the modern sense, although they were independent artisans from a legal point of view. The same characteristic applied to the membership of German consumers' cooperatives. The cooperative "ERMUNTERUNG" ("Encouragement"), which historians believe was the first consumers' cooperative in Germany, was founded at Chemnitz in 1845, by a group of workers, who were weavers and spinners. Both the Rochdale and the Chemnitz weavers had to struggle against the same miserable conditions, and they both rejected the existing economic system and the single-minded pursuit of profit. Both groups, the German and the British pioneers of consumers' cooperatives, were looking for a solution to the social question, not so much at the political level as through mutual aid between those who were suffering, by means of enterprises that were to follow new rules.

THE CONSTITUTION OF CONSUMERS' COOPERATIVES

The pioneers of the consumers' cooperative movement created enterprises whose constitutions were diametrically opposed to those of the private companies, which were also about to take on their final form in those days. The constitutions of consumers' cooperatives were dominated by two principles both embodying the idea of mutual aid, as opposed to principle of profit followed by ordinary companies. These were the principle of "one man, one vote" and the cooperative dividend based upon purchases by members.

Each member had only one vote in the Assembly to exclude the creation of new economic power, which might arise from a large share in the cooperatives' capital (83). This principle ensured equality between individuals and each member's individual inportance in the cooperative.

The principle of the cooperative dividend signified that the business proceeds would accrue to all members, according to their participation in the cooperative's activities. As anyone could join a consumers' cooperative, anyone could have a share in its proceeds.

This signified that there was a third way of sharing out profits, alongside the capitalist method, which assigned them to capital owners, and the socialist method which provided for workers' participation via producers' cooperatives. The cooperative dividend solved not only the apparently insoluble problem of how to distribute the surplus to a larger group of participants, but it also procured new members, new shareholders and thus new customers (84). The principle of the cooperative dividend was surely one of the most important factors in securing the success of consumers' cooperatives. It must not be forgotten, however, that the consumers' cooperatives also tackled social problems, as can be seen from a series of practical measures designed to improve the situation of the consumers, predominantly in the field of education. Consumers' cooperatives sold their goods only for cash, selling unadulterated wares at full weight – a business attitude that was by no means the rule in those days.

CONSUMERS' COOPERATIVES AND INDUSTRIAL COOPERATIVES

In Germany, the consumers' cooperative movement was predominantly a middle-class affair up to the time when it broke loose from the general middle-class movement. The rejection of the consumers' cooperatives by the early theoreticians of the workers movement inhibited their development among the working class and contributed to the fact that they were discovered late by organized labour. As close contacts developed between the consumers' cooperatives and the workers' movement in the nineties, disagreement flared up between consumers' cooperatives and middle-class cooperatives, as a result of which both groups separated. The consumers' cooperatives were expelled from the General Association ("Schultze-Delitzsch") at its congress in 1902 at Kreuznach, because of their close contacts with the Social-Democratic Party (the so-called "heresy tribunal" of Kreuznach!).

In 1894, 47 autonomous consumers' cooperatives founded the Wholesale Society of German Consumers' Cooperatives Ltd. ("Grosseinkaufsgesellschaft deutscher Konsumvereine mbH, GEG"). Some consumers' cooperatives even began to accept savings from their members, an operation that was facilitated by the fact that members could be credited with the amount of their cooperative dividend. This gave rise to a full-blooded conflict between consumers' cooperatives on one side, and traders' and credit cooperatives on the other. Propaganda went so far as to assert that consumers' cooperatives caused the ruin of the middle-classes.

Consumers' cooperatives had to leave the General Association because this organization of industrial cooperatives decided in favour of small retailers and against consumers' cooperatives. On top of this there were political conflicts. "Liberal bourgeois elements opposed socialist doctrinaires, and the middle-class representatives wanted to stay aloof from the working-class" (85). "As both cooperatives, from a sociological point of view, had their origin in different social classes, they exhibited contrasting development inclinations (86).

In 1903, German consumers' cooperatives founded their central association. This gave rise to a three-level-organization. At the lowest level were the local cooperatives, at the next the district associations, and at the top there was the Central Association, which organized a congress every year.

In 1903 altogether 666 consumers' cooperatives representing 573,000 members belonged to the Central Association; nevertheless, 251 more consumers' cooperatives with 248,000 members remained in the General Association ("Schulze-Delitzsch").

The new organization had a central purchasing agency, an independent auditing organization, educational arrangements for its personnel, a pension fund, and soon some participation in the sphere of insurance in the "Volksfürsorge" and the "Eigenhilfe Sachversicherung". At the local and district level as well as within the Wholesale Society, consumers' cooperatives maintained numerous establishments, bakeries, butchers' shops and meat factories, factories for cigarettes, alcoholic drinks and detergents, their own wine cellar and a deep-sea fishing fleet.

The enlargement of cooperative factories went parallel to certain ideas of the time, which aimed at a kind of cooperative Socialism or a cooperative Commonwealth (87). For a long time these ideas had been an undercurrent in the cooperative world, but they certainly contributed much to the foundation of cooperative factories. If one considers possible consequences of these ideas, there is only one thing that seems to be certain: consumers' cooperatives would never have been able to win support from workers, before and after the turn of the century, if they had not claimed to be the nucleus of a new and juster economic order. To achieve great things, one must be ready, after all, to transform an entire world (88).

CHRISTIAN CONSUMERS' COOPERATIVES

Alongside these two movements in German consumers' cooperation, the Socialist and the Schulze-Delitzsch branch, a third branch, the Christian consumers' cooperative movement, formed at this time. The increasing involvement of the workers' movement with the consumers' cooperatives caused the Centre Party and the Christian trade unions, which were closely related to it, and which had been founded about this time (1890), to build up their own Christian consumers' cooperatives. They proceeded first to the foundation of so-called "purchasing centres" for coal and potatoes, which were then transformed into genuine consumers' cooperatives with their own food shops.

Christian cooperatives chiefly originated in the provinces of Rhineland-Westphalia and Hesse-Nassau. The first Christian cooperative was founded at Mönchen-Gladbach in 1900. In 1902 the General Union of Christian trade unions in their congress at Munich recommended the foundation of consumers' cooperatives as an important means to improve the economic situation of workers.

They first of all thought of the foundation of trade unionist cooperatives with the idea of establishing a stronger link between trade union members and their organizations. At the demand of Peter Schlack, the leader of the national Christian trade unions the experiment was cut short as early as 1905. These trade union shops had too limited a success. Only after changing them into general cooperatives without any particular conditions on members did a larger movement start, which culminated in the foundation of the"Reichsverband Deutscher Konsumvereine" in 1913.

At that time Christian trade unions established the following rules for their consumers' cooperatives: both organizations had to work separately without interlocking positions at the top, the designation "trade unions" was to be dropped, and no trade union money was to be spent on acquiring cooperative shares (89). The cooperative movement was thus transformed into a pure consumers' organization, which was recognized as a necessary complement to their activities by Christian trade unions. Schlack characterized the relationship between Christian consumers' cooperatives and Christian trade unions at the trade union congress at Dresden in 1912, as follows: "While trade unions aim at an increase of their members' income, consumers' cooperatives aim at raising their purchasing power. The development of consumers' cooperatives has become indispensable for the working-class in these days of rising prices of food and other necessities. The congress of Christian trade unions recommends that all members of affiliated unions join consumers' cooperatives . . ." (90).

The congress of the Christian trade unions at Dortmund in 1926 culminated in great solidarity between Christian trade unions and consumers' cooperatives. On this occasion, it was pointed out that consumers' cooperatives provide the best means of bringing about co-ownership and joint participation by the workers as well as promoting economic democracy.

Cooperative societies are above all an organization of consumers and not of producers and therefore, they cannot simply conform to all demands of trade unions. Both are organizational forms of the working class, and they collaborate and help each other, retaining nevertheless their complete autonomy.

The "Reichsverband Deutscher Konsumvereine", as the Central Union of Christian consumers' cooperatives was called, built up its own purchasing centre, the "Grosseinkaufszentrale Deutscher Konsumvereine" mbH., which changed its name in 1923, into "GEPAG – Grosseinkaufs – und Produktions A. G. Deutscher Konsumvereine". It did not belong to the "AllgemeinerVerband" (General Association) which retained its middle-class character.

From now on people talked of the two "ideological branches" of consumers' cooperatives, namely of the (Socialist) branch at Hamburg ("Zentralverband") and the (Christian) branch at Cologne ("Reichsverband"). The political schism between the two branches had extremely grave consequences. There were now two seperate buying societies and their competing industrial undertakings. This also blocked the way towards a combination of cooperative forces within one big association. There was, besides, the antagonism of these towards the middle-class cooperatives, which either were not affiliated to any organization or remained with the General Association ("Allgemeiner Verband"). It must not be forgotten that the Hamburg branch was by far the stronger of the two with a membership ratio of about 4:1, as opposed to the Christian branch.

In spite of the close collaboration between the various pillars of both movements, i.e. the political parties, trade unions, cultural organizations and consumers' cooperatives, on the socialist side (where they comprised the "free trade unions" and the consumers' cooperatives of the "Zentralverband") as well as on the side of the "Centre Party" (with its Christian trade unions, auxiliary church organizations and consumers' cooperatives of the "Reichsverband"), both organizations retained until 1933, their genuine cooperative principles, viz. self-help and self-government. They had been founded as mutual-aid organizations for consumers and they retained this character, while adequately fulfilling their tasks.

THE DISSOLUTION OF CONSUMERS' COOPERATIVES IN THE THIRTIES

The Nazi party opposed all branches of the consumers' cooperative movement because of their democratic principles. The Nazi Party was to a large extent the political gathering ground for impoverished middle-class elements that eked out a living in the retail trade. These groups preferred to disguise their competitive jealousy under the cloak of political ideology. The Fighting Union of the Commercial Middle-classes ("Kampfbund des gewerblichen Mittelstandes") in particular, later called the National-Socialist Commerce and Trade Organization – NS-Hago ("Nationalistische Handels – und Gewerbeorganisation"), introduced primitive middle-class ideology into the Nazi programme, and this culminated in slogans like "destroy the slavery of debt" and "down with department stores and consumers' cooperatives".

From 1933 onwards the Nazis began to "adapt" the consumers' cooperatives. They were obliged to accept Nazi representatives on all executive organs of central associations, wholesale societies and local cooperatives. At a stroke, both branches, the socialist "Central Union" and the "Reichsverband" with their wholesale societies, were amalgamated into the "Reichsverband der Deutschen Verbrauchergenossenschaft e.V." in Berlin, and at the same time, the Nazis dissolved 73 consumers' cooperatives with 1,1 million members on the pretext that they were no longer viable.

They also ordered the cooperative savings establishments to be closed. In 1941 all consumers' cooperatives were finally dissoved. Shares were repaid to members at their nominal value, and the whole of the remaining property was transferred to the Community Fund of the German Labour Front ("Gemeinschaftswerk der deutschen Arbeitsfront"). Even the Austrian consumers' cooperatives and their wholesale society were dissolved. Enterprises and establishments of consumers' cooperatives were combined into 135 so-called 'Supply Rings", i.e. local retail chain stores, and the final purpose of this operation was the transfer of these shops into the hands of deserving war veterans. In the meantime these "Rings" offered good earnings to Nazi followers. The remnants of consumers' cooperatives continued to exist in this condition up to the end of the war.

THE REBUILDING OF THE CONSUMERS' COOPERATIVES

After the Second World War, stalwart cooperators founded the consumers' cooperatives afresh as non-party organizations without religious affinities, with one central association and a single great wholesale society, the GEG. Even after the membership had been rebuilt, it took some time, in fact until the early fifties, before the remaining property of former consumers' cooperatives could be restored to the new and rightful owners. The body Community Fund of the German Labour Front ceased to exist, and its property, as with all Nazi property, was confiscated by the Military Government. The "Supply Rings", it is true, continued in operation under trustees with the transfer of their assets into cooperative hands taking place over a period of years.

Chapter 7

RESTRUCTURING CONSUMERS' COOPERATIVES

In the early fifties in the wake of the Second World War a wave of rationalization measures swept over the wholesale and retail food trade, involving a considerable degree of concentration and fundamentally transforming the structures and market conditions in this sector in a single decade. This development has been ably described by Erich Batzer: "Wholesalers strengthened their position, vertical forms of organization were built up, new marketing techniques and sales concepts were developed within the framework of enlarged group structures, and finally the number and variety of articles offered increased" (91). This wave of rationalization also enforced a complete structural transformation of consumers' cooperatives as well as a new orientation in cooperative ideas.

We may characterize the transformation in food and luxury retailing as follows. Food retailing, an activity where almost atomistic competition had prevailed between innumerable small shops, became more and more oligopolistic in its market situation and forms of enterprise. This was the consequence of the reconstruction of large firms, multiple shops and the food sections of department shops. In the years following the monetary reform they expanded much more rapidly than the food trade as a whole. Their share in total food retailing sales rose from about 10%, in 1950 to almost 25% in the second half of the sixties. Large firms thus regained the market position in food retailing, which they had held at the beginning of the thirties (1932 = 22%), before the Nazi régime pushed them systematically into the background by means of its repressive measures against large retailing firms.

The restructuring of the food retail and wholesale trade proceeded largely from the fifties onwards as formerly independent wholesalers and retailers reorganized themselves into chains and groups. Generally such associations were based upon certain wholesalers or wholesale groups. The proportion of the market governed by these groups rose from 2%, in 1950 to about 50% in the middle of the sixties. Simultaneously the share in sales of unorganized wholesalers and retailers went down from about 66%, in 1950 to 2 or 3% over the same period.

From the legal point of view, these voluntary chains and groups are often nothing but working associations of independent dealers. From the point of view of industrial economics, however, they got beyond this stage long ago. They represent in fact large trade enterprises in statu nascendi, a transitional form of enterprise leading to large, and sometimes very large, multiple shop systems.

The form of organization adopted by these chains and rings is similar to that of large firms elsewhere in retailing. They are also built up vertically on several levels, with their own central wholesale agencies and purchasing centres. The economic power often lies on the purchasing side and this influence may grow in particular, if financial help is provided to the central organization of the chain. The central wholesale agency also has the tendency to join with other chains. It is already possible to foresee the day when the food and luxury trade will consist of only a few dozen big firms.

THE UNION OF GERMAN CONSUMERS' COOPERATIVES

German consumers' cooperatives took these changes into account in adapting their own structures to the new conditions. From the point of view of business economics, they are now a big new enterprise in the making, directed by the Union of German consumers' cooperatives ("Bund deutscher Konsumgenossenschaften"), which is the leading organization at the top level of the cooperative group.

The General Council of the Central Association of German consumers' cooperatives appointed in 1964 a "Reform Commission", presided over by Professor Dr. W. M. Kirsch, to work out proposals aimed at an improvement in the profitability of the entire system of consumers' cooperatives. The reform commission, therefore, had to take into account all the activities of the consumers' cooperatives in all their fields. In February 1967 the commission submitted its final report, which was then discussed in detail at a special congress. The debate resulted in the adoption of the reform proposals. It was decided to create a new central body for the consumers' cooperative movement, the "Bund Deutscher Konsumgenossenschaften" (The Union of German Consumers' Cooperation), which would be empowered to take decisions for the whole movement and to direct its activities. The "Bund" was itself created at the following congress in June, 1967. Since that time, it has been the leading organ of this group of enterprises, its task being the improvement of the performance of the consumers' cooperative community. The Central Association, which had hitherto represented the movement, was dissolved. Auditing activities were taken over by a special audit organization, the "Revisionsverband Deutscher Konsumgenossenschaften".

The new "Bund" is an attempt at concentration by merger, and represents a consistent development of the cooperative idea. Consumers' cooperatives right up to the Second World War retained an organizational structure which was a relic of the nineteenth century. Merely a cooperative association, within the framework of central societies and associations, was no longer sufficient as a form of organization, given the new conditions of competition. Consumers' cooperative associations had to be rebuilt in a more efficient way. This was only possible through a limitation of the autonomy of local cooperatives, through the transfer of certain powers of collaboration and through the surrender of policy-making functions to the new "Bund". By these acts of renunciation the individual societies have made it possible for the new head organization in Hamburg to develop new ideas for more rational business units and to introduce these at the local level.

The "Bund" represents a higher point of control designed to induce cooperative societies to behave uniformly and to operate jointly on the market. It is quite clear that there are parallels between their activities and new forms of cooperation in private trade. Nevertheless, the organizational structure of the new group is unique. The "Bund" is able to exercise its influence on enterprise planning and administration including finance, and the policy on the selecting of goods and investments of individual societies. It also has some say in the nomination of the managers. The foundation of the "Bund" is the prelude to the transforming of the German consumers' cooperative movement into a big and efficient group of enterprises.

Early in 1969 consumers' cooperatives gave proof of their new entrepreneurial intentions with regard to both their customers and the market by operating henceforth under the name of "co-op". Only too often the old trade-name "Konsum" evoked ideas in the minds of the general public that no longer corresponded to the new conditions.

TRANSFORMATION OF THE COOPERATIVE IDEA

Parallel to the restructuring of the forms of enterprise and business units, there was also a change in the motivation of consumers' cooperatives in the sixties. There were probably three chief reasons underlying this development. Because of the general rise in the standard of living, the cooperative ideal was no longer pre-eminent for members as had still been the case some years before. People no longer felt that the idea of mutual help corresponded to actual conditions, as there was no longer extreme misery. In an affluent society, when sheer necessity no longer obliges people to stick together, group consciousness gives way to more egotistical considerations. Besides, economic and social progress contributes to the increased isolation of individuals, and the area of community feeling and joint action will be perceptibly narrower

(92). It must not be supposed that this tendency is limited to the sixties. It should also be remembered that individual economic goals have always constituted a major source of motivation for cooperation within the consumers' cooperative movement.

As developed by the Rochdale pioneers the principle of the cooperative dividend linked to the purchases of members had always given a prominent position to this component of individualism. The second reason for the profaning of the cooperative idea according to many authors, is to be seen in the growth of cooperative enterprises as they develop into big concerns. Increasing growth no longer permits the collaboration of members to the same degree as before. The question of whether this is really a compelling reason is open to controversy. The decisive point seems to be that ways and means must be found to allow for increasing collaboration of members in spite of the growing dimensions of the cooperative concern.

The third reason for the decline of the cooperative idea in large membership circles must be attributed to the Rebate Law ("Rabattgesetz") of 1954, which forbade the payment of a cooperative dividend of more than three per cent. From this date onward the legislation only permitted the same rate as that granted by private retailers. As a consequence consumers' cooperatives have no longer been able to fulfil their commonweal tasks in furthering the interests of their members in the same way as before. They can now only act on behalf of consumers in general. This, of course, is a source of irritation for old cooperators. It took a long time until the new ideas were really understood and members accepted the new goals.

Moreover, the change in the market structure in food retailing also makes it more difficult to pursue commonweal aims, by applying the method of directly furthering the interests of members. This alteration of the market towards an oligopoly situation obliges the cooperative societies to become centres of "countervailing power", whenever they want to fulfil the task of looking after their members' interests (93). If consumers' cooperatives were to fail in their aims, their "meta-economic" purposes would remain an empty phrase (94).

Consumers' cooperatives cannot exercise countervailing power, if they maintain their former structures and if they continue to apply their old methods. In order to be able to wield real countervailing power, they must combine in vast cooperative concerns, and they are obliged to rationalize their business methods in the same way as private retailers do.

Furthermore, they will have to replace the old system of numerous small shops by a network of big self-service shops and supermarkets. This, in turn, implies that they will have to switch over to unrestricted trade and away from the principle of the high cooperative dividend to the principle of market regulation by means of relatively low prices. Even if the cooperative dividend had not been limited to 3%, viable countervailing power could only be exercised by a commonweal enterprise operating a price-regulating policy.

As long as the new structure of food retailing, with its new ways of behaviour and its new aims, fails to penetrate the consciousness of members, this kind of reorientation will lead to a weakening of links between members and cooperatives.

BUSINESS CONCENTRATION IN RETAILING

The reason for the concentration movement in retail business is to be found in mergers at the level of business units, as a transition is made to capital-intensive forms of marketing. The early fifties had seen a vast process of rationalization at the organizational level in retailing. It led to the advent of large self-service stores and super-markets. The transition to self-service shops coincided with a rise of wage costs and was made possible through progress in the packing industry.

As it happened, the increase in purchasing power of the large masses of the population tended towards a larger assortment of goods. Dealers went over from departmental selection of goods to a customer-oriented assortment.

The range of goods was no longer primarily determined by trade requirements (i.e. by specialization favouring an assortment of goods based on technical necessities), but rather by the desires of customers to buy, if possible, everything needed in a normal household in the same shop. More and more articles were introduced into the assortment of retailers, especially meat and fish products, which was made possible by the introduction of deep-freezing and special frozen foods.

To understand the revolution taking place before our eyes, we must recall that retail shops were only 20 to 40 square metres in size at the end of the twenties, and that they carried only about 1,000 articles. Today, the average sales space of self-service shops covers an area ten times as large. Very often their sales space is some 500 to 800 square metres (supermarkets), and their range extends to 4,000, or in the United States to 8,000 articles.

Self-service shops and supermarkets introduced a new form of competition: traditional price competition between retailers was complemented by competition between different forms of marketing. This required large investment, which was generally beyond the retailers' financial capabilities. They depended, therefore, upon financial aid from wholesale firms.

From the point of view of industrial economics, the transition to bigger self-service shops meant that a capital-intensive form of marketing was introduced. This meant that costs, which were fixed over a certain range, now became the determining ones, whether the firm operated at a high or low level of capacity. If overhead costs cannot be spread in the smallest possible fractions over sales, a capital-intensive firm is condemned to remain hopelessly unprofitable, no matter whether it is well equipped or whether its products and activities are good. All this had been different in the twenties and thirties. Small retail firms only had costs, which varied directly with an increase or decrease of their activities, leaving on one side the rather low rents and staff costs. In those days, many retailers could still afford to live quite comfortably according to the old maxim "small turnover and big mark-up".

Under the Nazi system this attitude was reinforced even more by a kind of licence system, which applied whenever new retail firms or multiple stores were founded. Today, however, retailing is strongly dominated by the principle "large turnover and low mark-up", so that the food trade is one of the rationalized branches of commerce. There can no longer be any question of exaggerated profit margins.

For wholesalers, who financed the wave of rationalization in retailing, it was necessary to combine retailers, with whom they were associated, into a chain, in order to organize sales activities more systematically. It would not otherwise have been possible to obtain the sales figures necessary for capital-intensive marketing. Retailers belonging to such a chain had to stick to a certain assortment of articles, certain methods of pricing, minimum purchases etc., while they were also relieved of certain functions to enable them to concentrate fully on sales activities. As a result chain-stores should be considered as multiple shop enterprises acting jointly on the market.

SELF-SERVICE IN CONSUMERS' COOPERATIVES

Consumers' cooperatives were pioneers of rationalization in the food retail and wholesale trade. The tendency towards concentration had already developed in the cooperative sector before the first world war, and it was reinforced in the fifties and sixties. This was a period when the number of consumers' cooperatives diminished considerably. Instead of mergers occasioned by financial requirements, combinations aiming at lower costs occurred frequently. At the end of the Second World War there were still around 320 independent consumers' cooperatives in the Federal Republic. The movement planned mergers to reduce this figure to less than 100. Parallel to concentration on the part of the cooperatives, there were measures of reorganization. The transition to self-service implied a considerable diminution in the number of shops, with sales being concentrated on the large self-service shops. While switching over to self-service, consumers' cooperatives also followed the general tendency in retailing by taking over more and more non-food articles. The co-op group thus entered a new market, the non-food sector, which not only represents higher margins than mere food retailing, but also covers a growing share in household budgets.

For that purpose the group "co-op" is building up a new section, consisting of self-service department-stores, consumers' markets, supermarkets and co-op shops in all parts of the Federal Republic. The administrative centre is at Kamen, from which the co-op shops and the new establishments are supplied with commodities. The GEG mail-order firm belongs to this group. It sells its articles by distributing catalogues, which may be obtained in co-op shops. There is, besides, a chain of furniture stores consisting of 40 separate stores.

In future, the chief outlet for commodities sold by the co-op group will consist of large stores for food and other articles, i.e. in supermarkets, co-op centres and self-service department stores with more than 10,000 square metres of sales space. Local consumers' cooperatives participate in financing the required investment, which amounts to about 10 to 15 million D-Mark per department store. Up to 1975 an expansion of consumption goods sales to more than 600 million D-Marks is envisaged.

CO-OP WAREHOUSE SYSTEM AND PRODUCTION PLANTS

The co-op group is not only transforming its network of shops and extending its non-food business, but it is also enlarging its warehouse and supply system. Following the example of foreign consumers' cooperatives, it is about to establish a system of one-level regional warehouses, which are to replace the two-level central warehouses existing up to now. At the same time regional warehouses will also take over certain purchasing functions, transport operations and accounting systems for affiliated consumers' cooperatives.

The group has its own high quality production plants. Before even the turn of the century many consumers' cooperatives possessed their own factories at local and supra-regional level. Today more than 30 supra-regional plants are administered by the GEG. The co-op group now owns six meat factories, a fish distribution centre at Bremerhaven and a series of regional luxury goods shops. Besides this, there are factories for preserving vegetables and fruit, a brandy and spirits factory, wine-cellars, a plant for roasting coffee, a cocoa and chocolate factory as well as cigarette factories.

Chapter 8

PROBLEMS OF CONSUMERS' COOPERATIVES

Since the transition to big shops and a large selection of goods retailing has required a large amount of capital for two reasons. Firstly, competition has increased considerably, and finance from internal funds through appropriate pricing is only available to a limited extent. Secondly, general affluence entails the necessity of improving continually upon the quality of the shop network.

PROBLEMS OF FINANCE

The days when the retail food trade required capital only every now and then, financing its stocks by short-term credit, are gone. Since the transition to capital-intensive methods of production and marketing, the problem of how to procure long-term capital arises again and again. New and continuously available ways of raising capital must, therefore, be found.

A considerable part of new capital required will always have to be owner's equity. The proportion of owner's equity to total capital is a guarantee against loss for outside capital. New capital can only be borrowed if and when owner's equity has been formed. The greater the risks of a particular branch, therefore, the higher the proportion the latter must be. This rule is important for retailing today.

These new financing needs, which the co-op group has to face today because of the transition to capital-intensive marketing, raise the problem of a reform of cooperative law. In its present legal form, the cooperative society does not possess a constant amount of owners' capital, for its is obliged to repay shares to members, who leave the society. Whenever new members join the cooperative society, owner's equity increases, and whenever someone leaves the cooperative, it decreases automatically. In the present legal set-up, therefore, the cooperative society does not offer a good framework for capital-intensive enterprises.

This was the lesson to be drawn from the failure of almost all attempts to introduce industrial production cooperatives into business life (95). For the same reason housing societies did not flourish either. It was for this reason that larger housing societies preferred company law, while retaining their public utility character. Often cooperatives of a capital-intensive nature succeeded in spite of their legal form, only because they fulfilled certain tasks prescribed by public authorities. For instance, many cooperative societies retain practically monopoly positions in certain areas of agricultural policy.

MEMBER AND NON-MEMBER BUSINESS

The "Rebate Law" of 1954, which has been mentioned above, created many more difficulties. With this law there was no longer any incentive to enter a cooperative to acquire a right to a considerable cooperative dividend.

The offer made to the consumers' cooperatives at that time, to return instead to the principle of selling only to members, was in fact no real alternative. The proposal was based upon an old theory called the "principle of organic economy", which was refuted by Draheim; according to that theory, consumers' cooperatives had directly to aid their members' households by offering a better supply of commodities (96). Cooperative societies are thus only supposed to act as auxiliary organizations or as organisms designed to support their members. This thesis still applies perhaps to smaller middle-class purchasing or marketing cooperatives, but it is not applicable to consumers' cooperatives working in large enterprises.

It is quite certain that a return solely to membership business would never have been possible, in view of the complete transformation of income conditions and of larger purchasing possibilities, taking into account the change to self-service shops and large stores and the profaning of the cooperative idea. High cooperative dividends – in some cases as high as 12% – had already been controversial in the cooperative world at the turn of the century, for they normally presupposed relatively high prices, so that the retail price level was influenced little if at all.

At that time, the supply aspect was still predominant, with pricing policy in the background. Under the umbrella of relatively high prices, which were the consequence of high cooperative dividends, many small private retailers could live comfortably following the principle of "small turnover and high mark-up".

A high cooperative dividend is only compatible with business confined to members. Because of non-membership business, the "auxiliary and complementary functions were discarded in favour of the entrepreneurial" (97). High prices and high cooperative dividends are not compatible with a modern market economy, with price-conscious consumers and hard-hitting competition from mail-order firms, discount houses, chain stores and rings. In view of lower margins, it would hardly be possible today for many consumers' cooperatives to pay dividends higher than 3% for prolonged periods.

Even if rebates of more than 3% had been possible and had been paid, consumers' cooperatives could hardly have recruited enough new members by these methods to be able to adapt their basic proprietary capital time and again to business requirements. The co-operative method of obtaining fresh owner's equity, by recruiting new members by means of a high cooperative dividend on purchases, would be rather expensive today.

THE CO-OP REAL ESTATE FUND

As yet consumers' cooperatives had applied makeshift solutions to their problem of how to obtain proprietary capital, and these in no way constituted a real solution. It would only have been possible to continue to apply such makeshift solutions, if it could have been supposed that capital requirements were temporary and transitional, and that the cooperatives could in the main rely on internal funds.

So far new sources of finance have been created solely through the foundation of real estate fund. An investor need not finance all the required investment out of internal funds. The investment can be undertaken by friendly or subsidiary sister companies and rented from them. This is the case, for instance, with the real estate funds. These subsidiary companies are then able to issue shares to the general public to build up new capital. In this way, the mother company can obtain additional funds through the subsidiaries.

The co-op real estate fund has been charged by the co-op group with the task of obtaining the necessary investment funds for the construction of new buildings, especially for the foundation of large new stores. At the same time it offers an opportunity to savers to participate in building up capital in real estate, by negotiating in particular on their behalf for the advantages of good business and housing sites.

The fund issues to the general public certificates representing shares in capital values of the fund. They bear interest in proportion to the profits different investments yield; and they benefit from the increase in values in the field of real estate. Money obtained by the fund in this way is used for the construction of shopping centres, groups of shops or other buildings, which are then leased to various cooperatives, to the Wholesale Society (GEG) and even to other firms. In order to distribute the risks as reasonably as possible, the fund does not limit its activities to projects launched by consumers' cooperatives. This system of indirect formation of owner's equity through the medium of real estate funds – a system which has already been applied successfully in other areas – is certainly capable of further extension with similar positive results.

OTHER SOURCES OF FINANCE

In this context we must also mention the share of GEG in the International Co-operative Bank in Basle. 26 consumers' cooperatives, cooperative wholesale societies, cooperative banks and insurance companies from 13 western countries hold shares in this bank. It promotes international cooperation among consumers' cooperatives, and its task is, inter alia, to obtain access to the Swiss capital market for consumers' cooperatives.

Cooperative societies, however, have so far chiefly covered their capital requirements for their vast rationalization measures, by recovering a good deal of the capital they had invested outside retailing. In 1964, for instance, they sold to the trade unions their shares in the "Bank für Gemeinwirtschaft", shares which had shown considerable growth. In 1968 the consumers' cooperatives also sold some shares in enterprises of the group "Volksfürsorge", some of the shares going to the Bank.

There will certainly be other opportunities in the future for the sale of industrial establishments to enable consumers' cooperatives to invest the proceeds in their network of shops and their warehouse system. Because of its great purchasing power the co-op group very often realizes much more favourable prices than its own establishments could ever hope to yield (98).

MODIFICATION OF THE LEGAL FORM

Problems of finance for the co-op group necessitate new ways of acquiring owner's equity, whenever it may be required. Modifications of cooperative law have already been envisaged in order to remove existing obstacles in the way of consumers' cooperatives obtaining proprietary capital, and to bring about equality in the conditions of competition vis-à-vis private firms.

The "Bund" (Union of German Consumers' Cooperatives) has already asked for expert opinions on the possibilities of reforms in company law and cooperative law. In 1969/70, a Reform Commission on cooperative law examined the question, and in the spring of 1970 it submitted proposals for a modification of cooperative law to the responsible cooperative organs. The legislator is no longer obliged to heed middle-class difficulties, considering that large enterprises dominate retail trade today in any case. All legal limitations impeding the development of consumers' cooperatives may, therefore, be dropped.

The legal form of the cooperative must be so altered as to make allowance for both the needs, which confront consumers' cooperatives at present. If today the co-op group wants to fulfil its task as a real commonweal enterprise defending consumers' interests, it can only do so as a large-scale enterprise. Only large firms are able to act as an efficient instrument for a policy of structural reform and competition in the interests of the consumer. Secondly, the group can only completely fulfil its task if it no longer acts, primarily, on behalf of its members, but is active in the interests of the general public.

This it can do by exercising a regulative influence on the market, aiming at low prices, high quality and good service. If there are no longer any exaggerated margins in retailing, especially in the food sector, this is certainly due to a very large extent, to the commonweal activity of the co-op group with its use of "countervailing power". Its central task consists in this function rather than in directly furthering the interests of members. The legal form of the cooperative society should be adapted to this change in its rôle.

CO-OP JOINT STOCK COMPANIES

Modifications of cooperative law as proposed by the Reform Commission, will very probably not be realizable within the next few years because of the political situation. Many responsible men within the union of German consumers' cooperatives have, therefore, asked themselves whether it would be appropriate to renounce the cooperative form altogether and to transform the cooperatives into a group of joint-stock companies.

If the cooperative law is not modified, a thorough-going and durable solution to the problems of finance can only be found by switching over to company law.

It must not be overlooked that those commonweal enterprises that functioned best have always been joint-stock companies. When Adolf von Elm suggested in 1910, that the trade unions and the consumers' cooperatives should adopt the form of a joint-stock company for the "Volksfürsorge" insurance institution, he recommended this because his experience with producers' societies as a cooperative form had been negative, and also because, as a founder and manager of the successful Hamburg cooperative "Produktion", he had come to know the limits of the cooperative society.

Company law çonfers one very substantial advantage. A joint-stock company can always raise new capital whenever it is wanted. A group of efficient retail and wholesale companies in a joint-stock firm would certainly find a market for its shares. The group is very well known in Germany, and the shares of department stores are anyway rare on the German capital market. Besides, co-op shares fit in very well with the widely publicized policy on capital ownership. A transformation of consumers' cooperatives into a joint-stock company oriented towards the public interest could certainly count on the sympathy of the public.

It would certainly be possible to change consumers' cooperatives into joint-stock companies without renouncing the commonweal purposes of consumers' societies. It is not a matter of great concern which final form is chosen, though there are many differing possibilities. It might be possible to establish the commonweal purpose in the statutes. As far as the board of directors is concerned, certain groups could hold the right to delegate their representatives who would guarantee the observance of the commonweal aims. Using the system of preferred stock without voting rights, it is possible to regulate voting rights in such a way as to make takeover by an outside group impossible.

The transformation into a commonweal joint-stock company would offer an opportunity to the co-op group to become more efficient and to carry out a commonweal business policy on behalf of consumers. The successful achievements of commonweal enterprises, which have assumed joint-stock form, show that business policy need not be prejudiced by the form an enterprise adopts.

Chapter 9

THE "VOLKSFÜRSORGE" GROUP

Every human society aims at security in its achievements. Thus cooperative societies joined together from an early date in order to assist people experiencing difficulties. The idea of cooperative assistance was behind the foundation of the first genuine insurance company in Germany, the "General Fire Fund" ("Generalfeuerkasse") of Hamburg, in 1676. This was a public insurance company with a structure based upon company law (99). At the same, there was an extension of State legislation to cover insurance companies, an act showing that governments felt it necessary to take measures to promote public welfare. Soon, private expectations about the provision of aid in case of need led to an extension of insurance into other areas, as, for instance, life insurance.

German insurance companies still show that both legal forms can overlap, for on one side there are legal pension and sickness insurance funds, 70 public law institutions and 125 large mutual aid insurance associations, surrounded by about 8,000 small friendly-societies. On the other side, there are only 165 joint-stock companies in the private capitalist sector, the majority of which carry on business to make profits.

Workers' organizations also approved of the idea of mutual aid between their members and so they began to found insurance societies. The idea of collective insurance has a common origin to that of trade unions and cooperative societies in the principle of mutual aid. Group solidarity goes well with measures of mutual assurances to ward off dangers which threaten. A social mission, therefore, derives from the idea of collective insurance.

SHORTCOMINGS IN EVERYDAY INSURANCE

In the early years of this century insurance operations, as it affected the man in the street through life assurance for sums of up to 2,000 Marks, failed to meet the social need of mutual assurance. It was no more a means of covering risks. On the contrary, for the lower classes, an insurance contract had in itself become a risk that could hardly be calculated (100).

The first life insurance companies in Germany were founded in the 19th century, according to the principles of friendly societies, which were based on mutual aid. It seemed appropriate for this form of enterprise to be based on the cooperative principle of mutual aid. It was only from the second half of the 19th century onwards that life and general insurance appealed to larger groups of the population, and joint-stock companies also began to enter the field. What favoured the sales of insurance policies was the fact that the standard of living had increased, and that future needs began to loom much larger in the eyes of ever increasing sections of the population. The need for insurance protection increases with growing standards of living. As soon as subsistence and daily needs are met, there develop secondary future needs that increasingly become as compelling as subsistence and daily wants at a low level of economic welfare. The insurance principle was also popularized by social legislation, beginning with the law about sickness insurance of 1883, and affected larger groups of the population.

Although insurance companies were already at the beginning of this century subject to far-reaching legislation, very unsatisfactory conditions had prevailed throughout the second half of the nineteenth century in those insurance activities intended to satisfy the needs of workers. Conditions in small-scale general assurance soon became notoriously bad, a fact which provoked discussions both broadly and at a scientific level.

Public criticism at the time chiefly attacked certain extreme business methods: the premium level was inflated by exaggerated expenditure on canvassing and administration, by excessive dividends to shareholders, and by other payments to members of the board of directors and the management. This was possible by means of enormously increased mark-ups superimposed upon the mathematically calculated net premium level. These mark-ups reached as much as 74%.

Criticism was also directed at the methods applied in the business. Real gangster methods were rampant, especially in the field of recruiting new clients. Insurance companies' agents were required to recruit a certain minimum number of people and so they promised almost anything, despite the fact that these promises could never be kept by their companies. These contracts above all contained a clause according to which the sum insured would be lost without compensation on the failure to pay the premium.

All the critics were unanimous in recognizing that small life-insurance would always be relatively more expensive than large life-insurance business as expenditure per client is the same. This, however, would not exclude the obligation to counteract the sheer exploitation of helpless groups of the population. Critics demanded a reform of small-scale insurance to effect a reduction in premiums and fairer methods and contract conditions. Above all, it should no longer be permissible for premium payments to be forfeited.

At that time many proposals aimed at an improvement in these conditions and a realization of the reforms were submitted to the public authorities. Among these reform proposals, the most remarkable was that of the president of the "Kaiserliches Aufsichtsamt", Dr. Gruner, who suggested that these abuses might be fought not through new legislation, but by the competition of an insurance company that would work fairly on behalf of its insured. What he actually wrote was this: "If it were possible to create an insurance enterprise in Germany that would offer absolute security and enjoy a good reputation, surpassing that of private companies, while enjoying the same confidence as a State institution does, and if this new institution, while preserving its character as a private business, would use its wide network of agents for propaganda purposes in the best style and in the best sense of the word – if all these conditions were fulfilled, small-scale insurance, provided that there is really a need for it, would not only expand to the greatest possible extent, but would also reach a high degree of perfection" (101). His suggestions were addressed to the private life insurance companies, which he wanted to persuade to found a large general everyday insurance company. He did not, however, succeed in persuading them. The private insurance companies rejected the suggestion aimed, they thought, at eliminating their own profits through one of their subsidiaries. Instead, somewhat later, the consumers' cooperatives and the trade unions jointly founded such an enterprise.

THE FOUNDATION OF THE "VOLKSFÜRSORGE"

Trade unions and consumers' cooperatives had already been discussing this subject for some time. In 1905 a proposal was made at the trade union congress in Cologne by the Central Association of Office Employees and the German Tobacco Workers' Union to abolish abuses in small-scale insurance by appropriate measures.

The trade unions wanted to protect the working class against further loss, for the largest group of subscribers to general everyday insurance arangements were workers. The discussion went on for some years, up to 1911, by which time clear ideas of reform had crystallized within the workers' movement. At a joint meeting of the Central Association of German Consumers' Cooperatives and of the General Commission of the Free Trade Unions, the latter suggested that a joint enterprise might be set up to provide small-scale insurance (102). The General Secretary of the Central Association of German Consumers' Cooperatives, Heinrich Kaufmann, declared himself ready to prepare a first memorandum on the subject. A joint study group was formed, in which the trade unions delegates were Gustav Bauer and Theodor Leipart and the delegates of the consumers' cooperatives were Heinrich Kaufmann, Adolf von Elm and Heinrich Lorenz. This group drew up draft statutes, which were approved by the representatives of trade unions and consumers' cooperatives. The study group initiated negotiations with the president of the Imperial Control Office ("Kaiserliches Aufsichtsamt"), who facilitated the foundation of the "Volksfürsorge" by rapidly authorizing its admission to insurance business.

In this context, a digression may not be without interest, because it shows the kind of hostility confronting the first commonweal enterprise of the working-class in the modern use of the term. Roused by the preparations being made for the foundation of the Volksfürsorge, the insurance interests tried to exercise as much pressure as possible on the Imperial Control Office, to persuade it to refuse the authorization. When it had finally been granted, the acting president of the Association of Public Law Life Insurance Companies, the director general of the "Landschaft" (regional mortgage company) of Eastern Prussia and "Geheimer Regierungsrat" ("Privy Councillor") Kapp, challenged the president of the Imperial Control Office, Dr. Gruner to a duel by pistol. The duel never, of course, took place. In passing it may be noted that the director general of the "Landschaft", Kapp, was the same man who in 1920 started the so-called "Kapp Putsch" against the Republican government, a rebellion which was to break down in face of the general strike proclaimed by the trade unions.

For these practical reasons the founders of the "Volksfürsorge" chose the form of a joint-stock company for their enterprise. Up to that time this form of modern business had been misused often in the field of insurance. Nevertheless, trade unions and consumers' cooperatives availed themselves of this legal structure, because it was the most practical of all the forms of business in question. As was soon to become evident, it was possible to breathe a social spirit into this legal form. So that the "Volksfürsorge" could always work towards its goal, dealings in the shares on the stock exchange were forbidden, the sale of shares required the authorization of the other shareholders and dividend payments were limited.

The most important and all-embracing task of the new enterprise was to put at the disposal of poorer people cheaper and better insurance protection than had been so far available, and to look out for new methods in general insurance. As a means of realizing these aims, it not only gave proof of thrift and economic methods in its business administration, but it also used the well-tried organizational apparatus of trade unions and consumers' cooperatives. Both founder organizations took responsibility for the recruitment of new members and of the collection of premiums by means of the honorary activities of part-time cashiers etc. This system of collaboration, by activating members for the common task, guaranteed the rapid rise of a modern trade union enterprise and blocked all attempts by opponents to jeopardize the activities of the "Volksfürsorge".

The initially promising development of the young enterprise was soon impeded by the outbreak of the First World War and the ensuing inflation. In the following years, however, the "Volksfürsorge" recovered quickly. It became the biggest insurance company in Germany for small-scale life-insurance business. At the end of 1932 its contracts numbered more than 2 million, representing a total sum insured of 660 million Reichsmark.

The "Volksfürsorge" was always very quick to provide for special needs. During the First World War it introduced a wartime life-insurance. This provided unheard-of assistance for the widows and orphans of soldiers. It thus assumed a social obligation towards the families of dead soldiers, an obligation insufficiently observed by State and society in those days. Nor did the "Volksfürsorge" remain idle in the days of the great depression of the thirties. In 1931, it introduced a makeshift insurance for unemployed clients. A person who could no longer afford to pay his premium would nevertheless receive a certain sum in case of death, if he set aside a few pence for such an insurance. This was an important source of help in those days. After the currency reforms of 1923 and 1948 the "Volksfürsorge" also did a lot for its insured. It developed special plans for them in order to adapt their situation to the new conditions. In this way, they were better placed than those who were insured with other companies.

In May 1933, the "Volksfürsorge" – as was the case with all other organizations – was "adapted" to the new conditions by the Nazi régime, to be operated as an enterprise of the "Arbeitsfront" ("Labour Front").

THE "VOLKSFÜRSORGE" GROUP TODAY

When the Second World War was over, a new era began in the development of the "Volksfürsorge". After the promulgation of a special law by the Control Council the trade unions and the consumers' cooperatives were able to refound the "Volksfürsorge" in 1947 in Hamburg. To dissociate itself from the so-called "Volksfürsorge" of the Nazi régime with its bad reputation because of its unscrupulous practices, the new company called itself "Alte Volksfürsorge" ("the old Volksfürsorge") to remind the public that the new was in fact the old. From 1969 onwards, when its old reputation had once more been restored, it has returned to the old name "Volksfürsorge".

In spite of the difficult times after the Second World War, the "Volksfürsorge" was able to reconstruct its organizational set-up in a very short time. With the loss of the Eastern territories, it had lost a large part of its real estate assets, which had been situated there. The number of its agencies had also been reduced to less than half of what they had been. Nevertheless, the company was able to fulfil its obligations to its insured shortly after the catastrophe of war, and this was due to an organization that functioned rapidly and satisfactorily.

At the time of the currency reform of June 1948, the "Volksfürsorge" had to recognize that it had lost most of its assets, as a consequence of the war. Nevertheless, it sought to realize the best possible solution under the circumstances. It, therefore, asked the authorities for approval of a special plan offering greater advantages to the insured compared with the currency reform procedures of private companies. About $1\frac{3}{4}$ million people who were insured with the "Volksfürsorge" benefited from this scheme at the time.

In the fifties a new and fruitful development for this tradition-rich enterprise seemed to lie in administrative simplification and the creation of new business possibilities. The creation of a few standard premium lists served this latter purpose. The "Volksfürsorge" was soon able to register a great success in that area of small-scale life insurance policies as well as in the large; it was able to grant a bonus equal to 20% of the annual premium, for every full business year since the currency reform, and this in spite of the fact that premium rates were rather limited, and had not kept up with the increase in the general price level.

The "Volksfürsorge" continued to make voluntary supplementary payments on the life policies of former clients for a period beyond the term of the policy. Even in its capital investment policy the commonweal character of the "Volksfürsorge" found clear expression. Considerable funds, under very favourable terms, were mobilized for social housing purposes.

During the boom phase of the business cycle in the Federal Republic the rise of the company continued. The year 1958 proved to be a landmark in the history of the "Volksfürsorge". In the so-called "Operation Settlement", which had its origin in the transformation of small-scale life insurance policies according to the stipulations of the "Special Plan" for the currency reform, it was possible to settle 770,000 insurance contracts involving a total sum of 220 million D-Mark. This operation was an outstanding achievement in the history of German insurance both in its size as well as in its financial and organizational aspects.

At present as measured by the number of policies, the "Volksfürsorge" holds third position amongst German life insurance companies. The marketing organization assumes an oustanding importance, for it consists of more than 30,000 part-time workers and has enjoyed a great reputation ever since the foundation of the "Volksfürsorge". To a very large extent it consists of members or officials of trade unions and of consumers cooperatives, who are canvassing on behalf of their own enterprise and for their own ideas about what the modern society ought to look like. They look after the insured's interest with particular zeal. At the same time, this system contributes considerably to good canvassing activity for the insurance sector, and it also facilitates the collection of premiums with a minimum of expenses.

Soon after the foundation of the "Volksfürsorge" as an insurance company, many of the insured expressed the desire also to be able to have their property insured by the "Volksfürsorge". It is necessary to offer a wide range of insurances, if only to organize efficiently and to use fully the capacity of the network of representatives. For that reason, in 1925 the "Volksfürsorge" founded a sister institute, the "Sachversicherungsgesellschaft" (Property Insurance Company). This was also transferred to the Labour Front in 1933, and reestablished in 1947 along with the life insurance company.

This company called itself "Deutsche Sachversicherung Eigenhilfe Hamburg" until 1968. Since the 1st of January, 1969 it has taken the name "Volksfürsorge, Deutsche Sachversicherung". Its activities comprise various areas of accident insurance. The "Volksfürsorge" has two other subsidiaries, namely the "Volksfürsorge Rechtsschutzversicerung" ("Volksfürsorge" Insurance for Legal Protection) founded in 1968, and the "Hamburger Internationale Rückversicherung" (Hamburg International Reinsurance).

Chapter 10

THE "NEUE HEIMAT" GROUP

The third big concern in this category is the building group "Neue Heimat" ("New Home"). It consists, properly speaking, of two groups: one that is a friendly society or a public utility establishment, and a second that belongs to the commonweal group of enterprises. The holding company of public utility character is the "Neue Heimat Gemeinnützige Wohnungs – und Siedlunggesellschaft mbH" (New Home, Public Utility Housing and Settlement Company Ltd), in short, "Neue Heimat Wohnungsbau" (New Home and House Construction). The other holding company of a commonweal character and not subject to public utility legislation, is the "Neue Heimat Städtebau GmbH" (New Home and Town Building Society Ltd). Both holding societies have their central headquarters in Hamburg. The management of the housing society is also the management of the town construction society. Both groups are the property of the German trade unions.

THE PROBLEMS OF THE HOUSING MARKET

Before describing and evaluating the achievements of the "Neue Heimat", we must first explain the factual constraints and the institutional framework imposed upon public utility housing enterprises. The central dilemma in housing is the stability of the relationship between rents and wages, i.e. the rent level settles down at about 20 to 40% of net income of lower and middle-class households, unless the State intervenes. This relationship was already prevalent prior to the First World War in Germany as well as abroad. Some progress has been made in the meantime in building techniques, which led to cost reductions, but, generally speaking, this has not entailed any basic improvement in the relationship between income and rents. As a rule tenants benefited from cost reductions through quality improvements. The ratio of 20 to 40% of the income, therefore, still prevails today, at home and abroad. In practice, this means that workers' incomes are generally too low compared with rent requirements. Under these circumstances, lower income groups can only afford housing that corresponds to current expectations, if the family disposes of several incomes.

This dilemma is not caused by economic factors, but by technical conditions. Whereas mechanized or automated production techniques are being applied almost everywhere else, manual and individual production predominates in construction in most cases. The relationship between wages and rents will, in principle, only improve when modern mass production methods are applied to house building. Until then the State will have to intervene by granting subsidies so as to bring about tolerable conditions, such that lower income classes will also be able to live in flats meeting modern standards.

Three categories of State interventions and subsidies, which are applied in ever varying combinations, can be distinguished in the housing market.

(a) State Legislation On Rent (Rent Control)

During and after the First World War, the level of rent was fixed by legislation or by administrative measures in most European countries. The result was a slower increase in rents by comparison with other prices and wages. The further outcome was that the ratio between rents and wages decreased, until by the early fifties rents were between 5 and 8% of wages. Simultaneously housing property became unprofitable. Building activity declined. In some countries, e.g. France, landlords had for some time not been able to carry out necessary repair work. After the Second World War in particular, it was clearly seen that rent control, which had been maintained for several decades, was leading to the decay of cities and to the depreciation of the capital stock invested in housing.

(b) Subsidizing House Building (Subsidizing the Commodity)

If, in spite of rent control and in the face of a rising of prices and wages elsewhere houses are nevertheless to be built, there are only two alternatives: either public authorities must begin to construct houses on their own account and bear the resulting deficit, or they must subsidize private house construction. The latter policy was adopted in the Federal Republic in the fifties on a large scale.

Landlords received loans or interest subsidies from public funds, on condition that they quoted rents based on costs. In such a way rents were kept relatively low. In most cases, the grant of public funds was conditional upon a further clause to be observed by landlords. They had to give newly-built flats, in the first instance, only to certain groups of people belonging to categories determined by the State. In such a way it became possible to reconstruct and even enlarge cities, which had been destroyed during the war, in spite of rent control being maintained for old houses. This system, however, brought with it a number of disadvantages, to say nothing of the necessity of a continual injection of public funds and these led to its gradual abolition in the sixties. First of all, the level of rents no longer corresponded to market conditions, and secondly, the situation in the housing market was no longer transparent. Both constituted strong obstacles to the necessary mobility of labour. The resulting situation often led to sheer injustice. All over the place people who could easily afford free-market rents were living in flats that were heavily subsidized.

(c) Rent Subsidies (Subsidizing the Person)

For this reason, measures were taken in the sixties to abolish rent control and to limit the system of subsidizing housing through the method of subsidizing the good or object. These measures aimed at creating a free market in housing, which naturally resulted in higher levels of rent up to the point where the old ratio of 20 to 40% between wages and rents once more prevailed. At the same time a system of rent aids was introduced for lower income groups. Under this system those who, on a scale laid down by the legislator, earn too little in relation to family circumstances to pay for a suitable dwelling, will receive a rent subsidy. This new method of subsidizing the person conforms to market conditions and avoids social injustice. Lower income groups are thus enabled to live reasonably well. It will, of course, always remain somewhat controversial to say what percentage of the tenant's income corresponds to a reasonable rent.

Besides this central dilemma of housing, which public utility housing societies are also unable to eliminate, there are still a number of problems which they may help to solve, to correct or to offset.

In contrast to the difference between the level of rent and the wage level, which is largely due to technical reasons, these other problems are of an economic character. They are caused by inelasticities of supply and demand prevailing in the housing markets.

Housing offers an excellent example of an imperfect market. First of all, housing markets are subject to regional limitations. The commodity "housing" cannot be transported. Excess demand in one place cannot, therefore, be met by over-supply in others. Secondly, housing markets are highly inelastic, for supply can only react very slowly to demand conditions, because of long construction delays. Thirdly, migration is generally a one-sided affair from countryside to town. Under pre-industrial conditions, only 20% of the population lives in towns and 80% in villages, but after industrialization the percentages are reversed. In practice, this group of the population brings about a high demand for flats in congested areas throughout the entire period of industrialization. This tendency is somewhat restrained by the motor car, which permits workers to live at a greater distance from their place of work than before. There are, however, increasing needs for living space and comforts, as a consequence of a higher standard of living.

PUBLIC UTILITY HOUSING ENTERPRISES

These three factors together, namely inelasticity of supply, migration from the countryside to the towns and the increased demand especially in areas where migrants settled, frequently led to unjustifiably high profits for landlords and owners of real estate. Public utility enterprises were created to counteract the unjustified gains and social abuses originating from these three elements, a task in which they have shown success. The first enterprises of this type originated in a manner analogous to cooperative societies, i.e. against a background of bourgeois and conservative household traditions, and inspired by humanitarian feelings, social understanding, and a desire for reform. Such were the motives inspiring men of progressive outlook to try and combat wretched housing conditions and exorbitant rents during the last century, both conditions being aggravated by the population explosion.

With regard to the origin of public utility housing enterprises, we may roughly distinguish three phases. Around the middle of the nineteenth century there were isolated pioneer achievements. As soon as the cooperative movement had obtained a firm legislative basis, many housing societies were founded in the form of friendly societies, as mutual aid institutions. The third phase began when strong social forces, initially in the form of public associations and institutions, began to tackle this problem. Amongst them were social insurance bodies, and after the First World War to a large extent local authorities and municipalities, and, finally, regional States in Germany. Housing enterprises with the title "Heimstätten" (Homesteads) have their origin, for instance, in provincial housing societies of this period in Prussia. At the same time trade unions of various types also began to tackle this problem, and later industry and the churches became active.

In this way the prototype of a public utility housing enterprise developed. Behind its origin was the fact that the State had begun to assist the activities of cooperative mutual aid organizations. The essential characteristics of this type of enterprise are the following:

1. An obligation to construct housing for the people. Public utility housing societies must continually construct. They lose their public utility status as soon as they stop building and only administer their houses. Furthermore, they must concentrate on the construction of small dwellings for low-income groups.

2. They have to promote housing reform and to contribute to an improvement in the quality of housing beyond the standards which have so far been usual for these groups. Their housing standard is supposed to be an indication of modern decent housing standards.

3. They have to apply the principle of cost price. This means that public utility housing societies in fixing their rent levels must constantly refer to construction costs. Particular administrative edicts determine in detail how the respective rent is to be calculated on the basis of costs. Public utility housing enterprises must not make profits which arise through the shortage of houses (103).

4. The State controls their business activities. Public utility housing enterprises are supervised by government control agencies and have to submit their accounts to the relevant audit organizations.

5. Dividends are to be limited to 4% of the capital stock. The law ordains that public utility enterprises must not pay more than 4% interest on the capital provided by their owners.

6. There is to be the formation of social capital; i.e. the capital so formed is permanently employed for social purposes. Should the enterprise ever be dissolved, only the nominal value of the founders' capital will be repaid. All the more recently formed capital must be used entirely for public utility purposes.

The State supported these aspirations of the public utility enterprises for the first time in 1894 by special legislation at the federal (imperial) level. A large number of legislative measures were taken by the regional States and later adopted as federal legislation. These measures introduced financial advantages for governmental controls over public utility enterprises, so as to guarantee the observance of the legal rules by the management.

From an early date public utility housing enterprises formed large business units. The first large-scale public utility enterprise originated through an establishment founded by a social insurance body, and another enterprise was founded through the joint initiative of the State and the coal mining industry. A third had its origin in the transfer of industrial housing to public utility enterprises. The enterprise under discussion here, the "Neue Heimat", had its origin in earlier trade union housing societies of public utility character, amongst others the DEWOG founded in 1924.

THE HISTORY OF THE "NEUE HEIMAT"

As early as the sixties of the last century a number of housing cooperatives had been founded as the result of a recommendation of the first meeting of the workers' associations in Frankfurt (104). Their development, however, was jeopardized by the fact that the cooperative legislation of the time provided for unlimited liability of members for the debts of their cooperatives. Only later, in 1889, was the law modified so that members were only liable for the amount of their cooperative share. For technical reasons the form of a joint-stock company was chosen, when such enterprises were later founded. In 1924, when the great inflation had subsided, the shortage of houses after the First World War led to a wave of foundations of trade union housing societies. The DEWOG enterprise ("Deutsche Wohnungsfürsorge AG" – German Housing Provision Company) was founded jointly by the three leading trade union federations, the organizations of the workers, the employees and the civil servants and by the "Verband sozialer Baubetriebe – BsB" (Association of Social Construction Enterprises).

In 1924, in the State of Hesse, the GEWOBAG ("Gemeinnützige Wohnungsbau-AG Hessen und Hessen-Nassau" – Public Utility House Construction Company Hesse and Hesse-Nassau) had been founded, which had its counterpart in Bremen in the GEWOBA ("Gemeinnützige Wohnungsbau-Gemeinschaft der freien Gewerkschaften für Bremen und Umgebung" – Public Utility House Construction Community of the Free Trade Unions for Bremen and District). Elsewhere in the German Reich other trade union housing enterprises appeared, and the DEWOG acted as a holding company for all of them. In different parts of the country the DEWOG had five agencies, which had been built up as advisory institutions to counsel local trade union housing enterprises and which were slowly transformed into subsidiaries of the DEWOG. Advice was given especially on financial and technical matters, and DEWOG coordinated their joint work and founded new companies.

A centralized housing society was not formed, however, because construction does not adapt itself easily to centralized methods. At no time had the housing market been a unified one. On the contrary, it consists of very many different sectoral markets, and in each of these very varied conditions may prevail. In 1933, when the DEWOG group was expropriated for the benefit of the "Deutsche Arbeitsfront" ("German Labour Front" – an auxiliary Nazi organization recruiting compulsorily all workers and entrepreneurs), the group owned 80,000 dwellings, which had been built between 1925 and 1933, throughout Germany.

In 1924 employees' unions, affiliated to the federation of free trade unions, formed the GEHAG, the "Gemeinnützige Heimstätten Spar- und Bau-AG" ("Public Utility Home, Savings and Building Company"); this subsidiary of the DEWOG closely resembled the mother company. In 1929, right-wing unions formed the "Deutsche Heimbau Gemeinnützige Aktiengesellschaft" (The German Home Construction Public Utility Joint Stock Company). This was an organization formed by the employees' associations of the "Hirsch-

Duncker" group, which was a "yellow organization"). In the beginning of 1933, this company owned about 11,000 dwellings and 175 commercial premises. From 1924 to 1932, the GEHAG built more than 9,000 flats, of which 8,000 were to rent. The employees' organizations of the Weimar period had their own housing societies. In 1918 they founded the "Heimat" ("Home"), and another joint-stock company, the "Gemeinnützige AG für Angestelltenheimstätten" (Public Utility Joint Stock Company for Employees' Homes), the "GAGFAH". This company constructed altogether 53,500 dwellings up to the end of 1929, of which 32,000 were administered by the company itself.

During the Second World War, the greater part of the trade union houses was destroyed. What remained at the end of the war was administered by the military authorities under trusteeship, and only gradually restored to their owners, the trade unions.

The first construction company to be released from allied trusteeship was the "Neue Heimat Kassel" (New Home of Kassel). It may be called the nucleus of today's group "Neue Heimat".

At the time Heinrich Plett, who gave great impetus to social house building in post-war days, worked in Kassel. He formed the enterprise "Neue Heimat" when it was transferred to Hamburg. From 1954 to 1960 the central board of the trade union federation DBG transferred all former shares in housing societies, which had been returned to the federation, to the "Neue Heimat" in Hamburg. Today, this society is by far the largest amongst more than 2,000 public utility housing societies in the Federal Republic, administ ering more than 1% of the total stock of houses in the Federal Republic. Its fixed assets may be valued at more than 5 million D-Mark.

THE COMMONWEAL ACHIEVEMENTS OF THE "NEUE HEIMAT"

The activities of the "Neue Heimat" chiefly represent a struggle against exorbitant rents, as has been described above. Such rents come about, it will be remembered, because of migration, inelasticity of supply of houses and demands engendered by increasing standards of living. Commonweal enterprises must guide themselves by the relevant level of costs, and for that reason alone they cannot profit from particular market situations. On the other hand private landlords will base their rent calculations upon specific construction costs. They always fix their rents with reference to the rents of recently built houses, i.e. the most expensive houses, taking some account of the lower value of the old houses as opposed to the new.

Public utility housing societies quote rents corresponding to the cost level of the year of construction plus administrative costs authorized by the State. In doing so, they are acting as a regulative force on the market while conforming to the principles of the market economy.

The "Neue Heimat" does not only have a regulative effect with regard to prices and quantities of housing, but also has an important influence in a social and qualitative sense upon the supply of housing. It does so, first of all, by furthering housing reform, according to the law on public utility housing and it improves the quality of houses beyond what has so far been customary for the lower and middle income groups.

Public utility housing societies have contributed a great deal towards the new standard of housing, with the result that hardly any flats are built today without a bathroom, and no blocks of houses without lawns and children's playgrounds. These societies set standards by which others have to abide.

Again, in many towns the "Neue Heimat" renounces its right to choose its own tenants by putting its new flats at the disposal of municipalities and urban housing authorities, who allocate them. In doing so, the "Neue Heimat" helps to mitigate housing shortages. Private landlords, on the other hand only choose the most creditworthy and quiet tenants in most cases. The "Neue Heimat" puts its flats at the disposal of other groups, for instance of families with many children, and thus increases the supply of housing for people who would otherwise encounter difficulties in obtaining decent housing.

An essential contribution to a qualitative improvement of the housing supply is to be seen in the fact that the "Neue Heimat" grants in effect permanent rights to its tenants. Provided the tenants do not carelessly infringe their contracts, they enjoy absolute security of tenancy and are protected against arbitrary measures. Furthermore, on account of the trade unions, the "Neue Heimat" has pledged itself to allow tenants, who are the victims of lock-outs or are involved in strikes, to postpone payment of their rents.

TRANSITION TO THE CONSTRUCTION OF TOWNS

During the fifties the "Neue Heimat" carried out its construction projects to satisfy the most urgent housing requirements. From the very beginning, it pursued an aim that was later to gain increasing importance, namely the realization of modern city construction concepts. In pursuing this goal, it created a great number of exemplary large housing complexes, mostly on the outskirts of large towns, interspersed with parks and provided with all the necessary communal amenities.

Included are groups of shops and even shopping centres, playgrounds and children's homes, cultural centres and all sorts of public institutions, as for instance, schools, medical centres, hospitals with nurses' homes, sports fields and recreation grounds, homes for apprentices and students, old people's homes and houses for disabled persons. The company avails itself of a number of eminent architects of international renown; it will suffice to quote the names of Professor Ernst May, permanent architectural consultant for town construction, Werner Hebebrand and Alvar Alto.

True to its commonweal principles of building houses, which fully meet people's needs, the "Neue Heimat" is extending its activities from the creation of individual housing estates to comprehensive town development. A new era thus begins for the whole group, and there are already some outstanding achievements; the block of houses at "Kaiserslautern-Bänjerrück", the Berlin Hansa quarter, the modern living quarter "Neue Vahr" near Bremen, the garden-city "Elbhochufer" at Wedel (near Hamburg), the modern quarter of "Neu-Altona" in the city of Hamburg. Various other complexes are planned or are under construction, namely the commuter town Müchen-Perlach, the renovation of the area of St. George in Hamburg and the "Hollerstat" in Bremem.

In the field of housing, slum clearance for whole cities becomes more and more important. "The rôle to be fulfilled by housing construction can be termed the 'integration into city building systems'; in the future, because of ever faster changes in administration, in economic life and in the life of society, we shall have to create areas that are better planned than before" (105).

Apart from slum clearance, the "Neue Heimat" is also trying to revive the city centres in vast urban conglomerations, to build houses near the work-place, instead of moving out farther and farther into sub-urban areas, for although these residential areas outside the towns are well provided with green belts, they develop into mere dormitory towns.

"NEUE HEIMAT STÄDTEBAU" ("NEW HOME TOWN CONSTRUCTION")

To provide housing near the place of work the "Neue Heimat" has gradually developed the free commonweal enterprise "Neue Heimat Städtebau". This new undertaking constitutes a well thought-out tool, permitting the fulfilment of new obligations in town construction. Through this enterprise the group is able to carry out any housing project of any size with all its associated amenities, to carry out slum clearance as well as reorganize entire communities. "Our task is to create the necessary conditions in towns, municipalities and entire regions, to procure for the future the same opportunities for living, education and professional life for everybody in Germany. This means the same opportunities in work places, housing, educational facilities, entertainment, municipal and social establishments ... It is important to offer these amenities and all the opportunities they contain to everybody, if possible" (106).

The "Neue Heimat Städtebau" consists of eight regional subsidiaries for town construction, as well as large-scale housebuilding, and can only be carried out efficiently with a certain amount of decentralization. Only certain tasks such as finance, planning and the inauguration of large projects can be organized centrally. The "Neue Heimat Städtebau" comprises five holding companies as well as the "Gewerbebauträger GmbH" (Commercial Construction Ltd.) founded in 1962, a company that takes care of planning, financing and constructing commercial buildings, and the firm "Neue Heimat Kommunal" (New Home Municipalities), which was founded in 1964 and deals with planning, financing and constructing buildings for public administrations. In 1965 the "Beratungsgesellschaft für Gewerbebau" (Advisory Company for Commercial Construction) was added to the list of subsidiaries. The programme of the firm "Gewerbebauträger GmbH" covers groups of shops, shopping centres and hotels and even complete industrial installations (107). The firm "Neue Heimat Kommunal" constructs hospitals, kindergarten facilities, schools, universities, old-folk's homes and gymnasia for towns and local authorities.

If desired, the firm takes over all commercial, technical and organizational tasks and even the financing. Such a comprehensive service very often means that towns and local authorities have a chance to start such projects for the first time. Rationalization and prefabricated construction result in unparalleled advantages pricewise for these projects. Another subsidiary of the "Neue Heimat Städtebau" is the "Gesellschaft für Wohnungs und Siedlungwesen (GEWOS)" ("Society for Housing and Settlements – GEWOS"), a firm, which plans town construction. The GEWOS deals with market research, investigates the needs of the housing market concerned and establishes the planning basis for such activities.

A further subsidiary of the "Neue Heimat Städtebau" is the "Neue Heimat International". This firm holds shares in a number of foreign housing companies all over the world. It collates experiences in house construction in other countries and makes available to other countries German experience in this field. Through its own construction activities in Common Market countries, especially in France and Italy, it is helping to create new ways for the development of a common market in construction and housing. It gives advice to young states and allied trade unions in developing countries on questions of house construction and thus contributes to international aid in a special way.

REORGANIZATION OF THE CONSTRUCTION MARKET

A further commonweal task of the "Neue Heimat" consists in the reorganization of the building market, for only in this way will it be possible to create the conditions necessary to resolve the dilemma of high rents. As far as prefabricated houses are concerned, the "Neue Heimat" acts as a pioneer: about 40% of the total amount if its constructions consists of prefabricated units. Not only does this have an effect on construction price levels and on building time, but also conventional private construction firms will have to adopt prefabricated construction.

The reorganization of the building market towards these new methods does not signify that the days of the small independent entrepreneurs in the building sector are numbered. It only means that in future, there will be a more pronounced division of labour in the construction sphere between large building enterprises and small artisans. For many decades to come there will be a lot of work available for old-style artisans in slum clearance and the modernization of old property. Looked at as a whole, the structural policy measures of "Neue Heimat", whether in building garden cities or in slum clearance in large towns, are not directed against middle-class enterprises, as is so readily asserted. In its style and efficiency the group "Neue Heimat" is unique in Europe. From 1950 to 1970 the group built 350,000 dwellings, commercial shops and community amenities. Most of the enterprises in which the "Neue Heimat Städtebau" holds shares are the largest of their kind in Western Europe. The "Neue Heimat" has already constructed complete town areas for about 40,000 people in 10,000 dwellings, with all necessary complementary establishments, and it is preparing vast new projects, one of which will comprise 16,000 houses. The firm is able to carry out all the necessary basic research activities, including both structural and market research. The development and construction of entire areas of towns with all necessary community amenities can be planned and financed by means of the firm's own facilities.

Chapter 11

WORKERS' BANKS

The fourth large complex of enterprises belonging to the consumers' cooperatives and the trade unions are the workers' banks, amalgamated today into the "Bank für Gemeinwirtschaft" (The Commonweal Bank).

Commonweal activities in the banking sector are by no means a novelty. In Germany as early as 1850 there were numerous institutions resembling banks, including even small-scale banks run by groups of workers (108). The capital was put up in most cases by trade unions, trade unions federations or boards managing trade union property, a fact which explains the name "workers' banks". Besides, there already existed certain institutions similar to banks and maintained by consumers' cooperatives, their central associations or wholesale societies.

The fact underlying this historical development was the rather high subscription paid by members of German trade unions even before the First World War, a contribution equal on average to one hour's wage per week. Thanks to these contributions, trade unions were able to run efficient office staffs, to construct their own houses and schools, and, at the same time, to build up important reserves to be used whenever strikes arose.

The fact that they disposed of such considerable liquid funds, led, prior to the First World War, to the foundation of credit institutions or establishments very like them. Credit and savings' institutions, which had their origin before the First World War, can be divided into five categories, according to the goals that determined the area of their activities and their business:

1. savings, loan and life insurance funds,
2. savings banks of professional associations,
3. civil servants' banks,
4. consumers' cooperatives' savings banks,
5. trade union banks.

These five categories of monetary and credit institutions, which belonged to the trade unions or professional organizations, had no lasting effect, because they primarily followed the aims of the trade unions or consumers' cooperatives. Even from a technical banking point of view these five showed weaknesses and only under very special historical circumstances could they have shown some success. If they are mentioned briefly here, it is because such institutions even nowadays exist abroad, and because proposals are made time and again in this direction despite the experience of the past.

WORKERS' AND CIVIL SERVANTS' BANKS

With the aid of accumulated trade union funds, small savings banks and loan and friendly societies grew up to satisfy the daily needs of trade union organizations and their service departments. In most cases these bodies did not actively invest their money, but lent it to other insituations. They became redundant after the reform of 1909, when the network of savings banks grew larger. The tasks, that could have been fulfilled by such institutions, were now taken over by public and municipal savings banks. The trade union savings banks and the loan and friendly societies were no longer competitive as the large savings bank network quickly developed.

On the other hand, prior to the First World War, professional organizations similar to trade unions had founded savings banks of their own. In this way the "Deutsche Werkmeisterbund" (German Foremen's Association) founded a savings department, which was converted in 1907 into the "Deutsche Werkmeister-Sparbank AG, Düsseldorf" (German Foremen's Savings Bank, a joint-stock company); in like manner the "Deutschnationale Handlungsgehilfenverband" (The German National Association of Clerks) in Hamburg and the "Bund der technischen Angestellten und Beamten" (Union of Technical Employees and Civil Servants) founded in 1922 the "Industrie-Beamtensparbank eGmbH" (Industrial and Civil Servants' Savings Bank Ltd.).

It is a matter of institutions that cater for well-to-do groups of employees. Only such people were able to build up lasting savings accounts in those days. They, however, were confined in what they could do and this was the reason why these institutions remained small and unimportant.

At the time, a larger network of civil servants' banks developed, primarily in the guise of cooperatives societies. Even before the First World War, cooperative banks for civil servants had been founded. The chief reason was the impossibility of obtaining personal credit experienced by civil servants; nor did instalment credit yet exist. This was the reason why a mutual aid movement came into being among civil servants. Civil servants' banks, mostly connected with buying cooperatives, sprang up everywhere offering personal credits to their clients and receiving in turn savings deposits. The reform of the cooperative law at the beginning of the century facilitated the founding of these banks. This development ended in the twenties, when the civil servants' savings banks became a third branch of the credit cooperatives, alongside the Raiffeisen and the people's banks. Civil servants' banks had their own clearing network and their own central body affiliated to the "Cooperative Banking Association". This third branch of the credit cooperatives consisted in 1930 of 77 civil servants' banks but with a balance sheet of only 155 million Marks. In 1929 it collapsed almost overnight. A civil servants' bank in Berlin, the "Berliner Beamtenbank", which was not affiliated to the civil servants' banking system went into bankruptcy, and this created a crisis of confidence in civil servants' banks as a whole, and led to their insolvency.

The basic idea of mutual aid, which lay behind the savings and loan institutions of the trade unions as well as the savings banks of professional organizations and of civil servants' banks, could not be realized at all. The expectation, which had always been cherished, of being able to pay rank and file depositors by means of this kind of association, at a higher rate of interest than did other banks, and of offering at the same time cheaper credit to their members, was impracticable.

Cheaper credits cannot be offered, if the savings deposits on which they are based are more expensive to acquire. It should be remembered that, at this period, savings banks, credit cooperatives and insurance companies existed almost everywhere, trying to meet the needs of the "small man" and to extend their field of activities. It must not be forgotten either that the level of wages paid to workers and even to most civil servants at this time, remained as a rule well below the possible savings level, which was at the same time a bench-mark for credit rating.

Above all, however, savings and lending banks limited to specific groups of the population will remain inferior to other institutions that are not limited to specific groups. Institutions of this kind, and credit institutions in particular, which specialize on the basis of sociological considerations, can never offer the element of security necessary for a successful credit house. In these cases, the borrowers run all manner of risks and dangers, so that despite a great diversity of people, a proper spread of risks for both debtors and creditors is still lacking.

CONSUMERS' COOPERATIVES' SAVINGS BANKS

Like workers' organizations of all kinds, local consumers' cooperatives often formed savings banks of their own, one of the chief reasons being that they were doing hardly any business with other savings and private banks, which were oriented towards the middle-classes. The "Grosseinkaufsgesellschaft Deutscher Konsumgenossenschaften" (The Wholesale Society of German Consumers' Cooperatives) in Hamburg, which was related to the Free (Socialist) Trade Unions, initiated the founding of such a cooperative savings bank, which at the same time served as a central clearing department. The banking department of the wholesale society in Cologne, affiliated to the Christian Trade Unions, followed this example.

The chief purpose of establishing such collecting points for deposits lay in the attempt to obtain from members the necessary funds to finance the movement's own commercial and productive enterprises. The idea of outside finance comes naturally to an enterprise following the principle of just covering costs.

Savings departments were established to replace the principle of self-financing by a system of credits from members, who are at the same time customers of the enterprise. This is one of the decisive reasons why such cooperative collecting points for deposits were founded.

In applying these methods the German consumers' cooperatives were not alone. The consumers' cooperatives in Great Britain and in France also possessed such institutions. British consumers' cooperatives disposed in 1922 of deposits amounting to £14 million. The corresponding institution in the French consumers' cooperative movement had deposits of 60 million francs, while total deposits with the banking departments of the Wholesale Society GEG and GEPAG amounted in 1930 to 450 million Reichsmark.

Since the Second World War, German consumers' cooperatives have abstained from opening their own savings branches. It is difficult in retail trading to handle banking business alongside normal sales. The opposition of private business to consumers' cooperatives has receded, so that self-finance with the help of members is largely superfluous. Besides, this method can never fully replace internal funds. Capital procured from members has to be considered as external capital, and to equalize risks, a minimum of internal funds must exist to offset it.

Since the typical cooperative dividend has been abolished, there is no longer a real stimulus for members to maintain savings deposits with consumers' cooperatives. In earlier times members of consumers' cooperatives received around Easter a dividend equal to five, six, and sometimes even as much as eight per cent of their annual purchases. This rather high once-yearly payment had been a good opportunity to persuade members to leave the sum with consumers' cooperatives as a savings deposit.

TRADE UNION BANKS

The first pure trade union banks postdated the cooperative savings banks. The desire to manage their own funds dates right back to the beginning of German trade unions. Some speakers proposed this idea at the first German trade union congress in Erfurt in 1872 (109). Nevertheless, the trade unions approached this problem in a rather reluctant and hesitant way, so that a trade union bank was only founded after the First World War.

The Christian trade unions were the first to found a proper trade union bank, in the real sense of the word, in 1921. It was called the "Deutsche Volksbank AG" (The German People's Bank – a joint-stock company), which had its headquarters first in Berlin and later in Essen. 70% of the share capital belonged to the Christian consumers' cooperatives. This bank was also the first to go beyond the occupational framework, which had limited the business circle of most workers' savings banks, for instance, the Foremen's Savings Bank, the Industrial Civil Servants' Savings Bank and the Savings Bank of the German National Association of Clerks. Even the new Christian trade union bank remained within the sphere of the Christian workers' movement and never got beyond the size of a typical "house bank". Only in its investment business, did it go beyond the circle of its founders, by extending building credits to public utility housing societies. At the end of the twenties, the bank possessed six subsidiaries and more than 400 receiving points for savings bank deposits at the local public offices of the Christian trade unions. Its balance sheet reached 26 million Reichsmark in 1929.

The Hirsch-Duncker Trade Unions' Bank in Berlin-Zehlendorf, which was founded in 1923, also remained limited to the trade union domain and to the world of its ideas. It was called "Deutsche Wirtschaftsbank AG" (The German Economic Bank – a joint-stock company). Possessing, however, only a small number of members, this organization had little chance of developing.

As was the case with other commonweal enterprises, the management consisted of banking experts. The supervisory board, being occupied almost exclusively by leading personalities of the trade union and cooperative world, took its instructions from these individual organizations. In such a way, in spite of the de jure independence of these enterprises, a very close link was established between them and the organizations mentioned, a feature which guaranteed a consistent business policy. In the beginning, their charters considerably hindered the development of their business activities, with the result that they only fulfilled the functions of a pure "house bank". Later on, however, practical banking business led to an extension of their activities, so that the kind of business they were doing especially in the case of the free trade union "Arbeiterbank" could hardly be distinguished from that of private banks.

The bank of the free trade unions, viz. the "Bank der Arbeiter, Angestellten und Beamten AG" (The Bank of Workers, Employees and

Civil Servants – a joint-stock company) in Berlin, which had been founded in 1923, no longer served as a "house bank". Its founders were the German free trade union federation and the majority of free trade unions affiliated to it.

The development of the "Arbeiterbank", as it shortly came to be called, was a brilliant one. By 1931, this institution possessed 9 subsidiaries and 136 agencies. In this way, it became an important money collecting centre for all organizations belonging or related to the free trade union federation. Furthermore, the bank accepted deposits, on a large scale, from other organizations with whom it entertained business relations through shareholders, as for instance, the social insurance institutions, sickness funds, cultural and political organizations, the pension funds of trade unions and political parties. In such a way, the bank obtained a large number of deposits with different seasonal fluctuations, and this improved its liquidity considerably. The bank also made use of the trade unions' cashier network, in order to obtain savings accounts from individuals.

In the extension of credit, the bank's business was limited to enterprises related to the founders' organizations, especially to consumers' cooperatives, to enterprises in the social construction sector and to trade union housing enterprises. It granted credits to daily papers, printing offices and book-shops that maintained close relations with free trade unions. In doing so, it paid great attention to the necessity of security from the banking point of view, even in the case of enterprises connected with its founders.

Up to the end of the bank in 1933, its business activities went only reluctantly beyond the activities of the typical "house bank". The first enterprises and institutions unrelated to the founders' circle, but which nevertheless accepted the bank's loans, were legal and public institutions, social insurance organizations, sickness funds and municipal associations. In this way, the share of credit granted to workers' organizations diminished to 53,8% by the end of 1931.

In the case of deposits the situation was similar. The share of deposits coming from legal and public institutions rose, right up to the beginning of the world depression in 1929, to 56,6%, whereas the share from workers' organizations and enterprises fell to 39,3%. It is interesting to note that the balance sheet share of the banks own money deposits was rather high: in 1930 it reached almost 33%. This high ratio of liquidity must very probably be explained by the precautionary measures taken by the management and the supervisory board of the bank. On the other hand this high degree of liquidity hints at the difficulty this young institution had in obtaining good debtors during the short time of its existence. The social climate of the twenties, and later on the world depression, did not at all favour an extension of business in the industrial sector. When the Nazi Party took power, all the enterprises of the workers' organizations including all types of credit institutions, were expropriated, in most cases in favour of the "German Labour Front". In this way, the development of commonweal enterprises was precipitately disrupted for about 12 to 15 years.

Whereas the other enterprises, the consumers' cooperatives, the "Volksfürsorge" and the "Neue Heimat", could start almost immediately after the Second World War at the point where their activity had been interrupted in 1933, this was only partly possible for the workers' banks. The institutions of the smaller trade unions were not revived at all, and the "Arbeiterbank" saw a new beginning, after the Second World War, as a commonweal business bank.

Chapter 12

THE "BANK FÜR GEMEINWIRTSCHAFT" (The Commonweal Bank)

Trade union banks of the Weimar Republic showed some tendency to universal banking activities, but they nevertheless chiefly did business with trade unions, remaining thus their so-called "house banks". Such a specialized bank, however, cannot, if left alone, function by itself, for the very existence of such a "house bank" contradicts the basic concept of a bank. A bank's function consists of accepting as much money as possible from as many people as possible with as varied repayment dates as possible and in making loans with as varied maturities as possible to as many customers as possible. A "house bank" deviates from these basic principles: it is effectively dealing with one customer on each side of its balance sheet. Every deviation from the law of large numbers diminishes liquidity and makes higher reserves indispensable to the detriment of profitability, and lower profitability tends to diminish security in banking operations. Yet, security and the availability of trade union funds on demand had provided the chief reason for the foundation of trade union banks.

A trade union bank cannot function, therefore, in the spirit of the founding organization, unless it is not simply a "house bank", but also does general banking business to a considerable extent, alongside its internal "house bank" operations. It will fulfil this latter function better, the smaller the "internal" business share in its total activities. Even the old "Bank der Arbeiter, Angestellten und Beamten" (Bank of Workers, Employees and Civil Servants) carried on some external business operations, alongside its internal activities; about 50% of all transactions – investment as well as deposits – were carried on with enterprises and persons that had no relationship whatsoever to the founding group. When, however, the "commonweal banks" were founded after the Second World War, general banking business was declared to be the absolute goal of their activities.

THE FOUNDATION OF THE "BANK FÜR GEMEINWIRTSCHAFT"

When trade unions and consumers' cooperatives started again as non-party joint associations after the Second World War, it appeared to be quite natural to choose a wider set of objectives for trade union banking, as had already been done for consumers' cooperatives. Commonweal enterprises adopted the form of general business banks at the disposal of the entire economic system, for investment as well as deposit business, and were designed to serve the whole population. This corresponded fully to the new trade union view conceived by Hans Böckler, that the workers' organizations should accept their full share of responsibility for the reconstruction of the German economy. In this spirit after the currency reform the trade unions, together with the consumers' cooperatives, founded six regional "Gemeinwirtschaftsbanken" (Commonweal Banks) in 1949 and 1950, which in 1953 were joined by the "Bank für Wirtschaft und Arbeit" (The Bank for Economy and Labour) in Berlin. It was not possible at that time to form a unified organization, in view of the anti-cartel laws, which were still valid in those days.

In December 1958, after the federal law allowing amalgamation among credit institutions, the six commonweal banks merged to form one common establishment, the "Bank für Gemeinwirtschaft AG" (The Commonweal Bank – a joint-stock company), in Frankfurt. This merger offered an opportunity for combining and simplifying the administrative services, for facilitating the supra-regional clearing operations for cash and liquidity, and for improving the ratio between loans and the bank's own capital. The merger also permitted a higher ratio of advances to total transactions. At the end of 1963 the bank altered its Berlin subsidiary, the "Bank für Wirtschaft und Arbeit zu Berlin AG", into an agency. This was done to show that the bank had complete confidence in the future economic and political stability of the city of Berlin.

The commonweal banks were soon able to gain a foothold in business life. Their central bank had a spectacularly rapid development after 1958.

The balance sheet sum increased relatively more rapidly than was the case with most other credit institutions. The original capital was enlarged to cope with the increased volume of business transactions and the share of the various shareholders was modified in the course of increasing the capital. At present the German trade union federation DGB and its affiliated trade unions hold 95% of the share capital while the rest is held by the Wholesale Society of German Consumers' Cooperatives (GEG) and the "Bank für Arbeit und Wirtschaft" in Vienna, in both of which the Frankfurt bank is a shareholder.

Business transactions of the bank take place in all fields of economic life since the re-establishment of the bank. About nine-tenths of the bank's business volume today is with private industry, commerce and trade, the public sector, private and public insurance companies, workers and employees and the liberal professions. As with any other business bank, it deals primarily with short and medium term deposit and credit operations and offers its customers all the normal range of banking services. Besides business in securities, the bank also enlarged its foreign trade operations and is today represented in all the important places in the world by correspondent banks.

The structure of the bank may be described by three concentric circles. The innermost circle is that of the "house bank" of the trade unions, consumers' cooperatives and commonweal enterprises. This circle is quite sound from a banking point of view, because of the differing liquidity requirements of the trade unions and of the commonweal enterprises, for the latter work in very different markets. Joint commonweal interests do not conflict with banking requirements. Today, the share of these customers in total business amounts to less than 10%.

Around this circle there is the second with the commonweal bank in its rôle as a general business bank. In recent years, the bank has enlarged its network of agencies to attract more small and medium-size customers than before.

Now, there is not a single big city in the Federal Republic, where the bank is not represented. It is for this reason that it now concentrates particular attention on the third circle, in the same way as other big banks do, namely to shareholding in other banks and specialized credit institutions, with the aim of rounding off its business activities. Initially such shares were predominantly held inside the country. But in the course of the past few years, the bank has also acquired a number of shares in foreign institutions.

BANK PARTNERSHIPS TO PROTECT SAVERS' AND CONSUMERS' INTERESTS

From the very beginning the commonweal banks served the general interests of savers and consumers. They, therefore, actively engaged in the consumer credit business from an early time, when other banks in the period after the 1948 currency reform served their old customers first and had few funds for such activities. For this purpose the commonweal bank founded as early as 1950 the "Westdeutsche Teilzahlungsbank G.m.b.H." (WTB), (The West German Instalment Credit Bank Ltd.) at Cologne, which is today one of the five biggest banks in this sector in the Federal Republic. Furthermore, the bank acquired a share holding in the "Warenkredit-Verkehrsbank G.m.b.H. (WKV), (Merchandise Credit Circulation Bank Ltd.) at Cologne, which also deals with instalment credits. For the last few years the bank has concentrated directly on small credits and the provision of loans. In this sector it still exercises a regulatory influence on prices.

From a very early time, the commonweal banks have promoted saving. Long before the government took active steps to foster a more equal distribution of property, the commonweal bank had already acquired a shareholding in the "Allgemeine Deutsche Investment-Gesellschaft" (ADIG), (The General German Investment Company), the first investment fund in Germany. Through the initiative of this company this form of investment certificates, which is well adapted to the needs of small savers, was introduced into Germany. In such a way the bank helped to bring about the conditions for widespread property formation based upon real assets.

In the autumn of 1965 the bank founded a special institution, designed to foster property ownership among workers. This is the "Bank für Sparanlagen und Vermögensbildung AG" (BSV), (The Bank for Savings and Property Formation – a joint-stock company) at Frankfurt. This bank was founded in partnership with the building workers' union ("Industriegewerkschaft Bau, Steine, Erden"), the impulse being the grant of a special bonus to foster property formation among workers in the construction sector. This bank, however, does not limit its activities to people employed in the construction sector, but is in fact at the disposal of all groups of the population.

The special characteristic of this bank is that the long-term savers have a share in the profits and they are also represented on the supervisory and on the advisory councils, thus participating in the administrative affairs. The supervisory council consists of fifteen people. Five posts are occupied by employees of the BSV, in accordance with the law on the internal constitution of business units ("Betriebsverfassungsgesetz"). Of the remaining ten posts only two are occupied by shareholders. The remaining eight representatives, the majority, are chosen from the long-term savers. The advisory council, which serves to promote closer contacts between the bank and investors, is additional to the legally prescribed council and is likewise constituted predominantly of savers. Its essential task consists in counselling the bank on all questions concerning property formation for workers, and on the investment of funds administered by the bank.

The bank has no agencies in an attempt to minimize costs and to guarantee high receipts for the savers. It employs, however, a modern computer system and simplified forms. The bank offers simple and convenient accountancy methods to undertakings, which are faced with new organizational problems because of the second law on property ("Zweites Vermögensbildungsgesetz") or tariff-treaties.

COOPERATION BETWEEN TRADE UNION BANKS

For several years the "Bank für Gemeinwirtschaft" has been fostering concentration among trade union and cooperative banks, which had hitherto worked in isolation (110). For a long time now, the bank has been collaborating with an Austrian sister institution, the "Bank für Arbeit und Wirtschaft AG" (The Bank for Labour and Economy) – a joint stock company in Vienna. Both are linked through reciprocal shareholding. Furthermore, the BfG acquired a 50% share in the Dutch trade union bank, the "Hollandse Koopmansbank Lippmann Rosenthal N.V." (Dutch Merchants' Bank) in Amsterdam, and an important holding in the bank of the Luxembourg trade unions, the "Banque de l'Union des Coopérateurs Luxembourgeois S.A." (Bank of the Union of Luxemburg Cooperatives) in Luxemburg. The BfG, moreover, cooperates closely with the bank of the Israeli trade unions, the bank "Hapoalim" in Tel Aviv.

Shares in a Swiss bank, the "Internationale Genossenschaftsbank A.B." (International Cooperative Bank) at Basle contribute towards international cooperative collaboration. Many cooperative societies and credit institutions, as well as trade union banks, from a large number of western countries hold shares in this bank. It establishes links between its members, affiliated cooperatives and other commonweal enterprises, and in this way furthers international cooperation. At the same time it remains at the disposal of all economic groups, in a manner similar to the "Bank für Gemeinwirtschaft". For this reason, the International Cooperative Bank has accepted shareholders from economic groups that have nothing to do with trade unions.

The banks mentioned here have sought, on their own initiative, closer contacts with the "Bank für Gemeinwirtschaft". For other banks related to cooperative societies or trade unions in those countries, the "Bank für Gemeinwirtschaft" constitutes a successful model of how to apply the principles of commonweal economy, and they are striving to imitate this example.

COOPERATION WITH PRIVATE BANKERS

The BfG cooperates with other institutions not only out of trade union and cooperative motives, but also out of general policy considerations. In doing so it is entering a new field, for it is trying to foster cooperation between small and large scale enterprise and between private and commonweal concerns (111).

The history of banking, at least on the continent of Europe, has been characterized by permanent mergers between smaller local and regional banks to bring about huge supra-regional banks with many branches. This has meant a certain death for the small private banker.

This, however, is not a desirable situation for banking. It is true that big banks are the appropriate form of banking for today. Nevertheless, the small banker's existence is justified too, and his services will gain even more importance in the future for two reasons.

First of all, there is in all western industrial societies a large and growing class of well-to-do people, of increasing affluence, who need competent advice on investing their money assets, and who are quite ready to pay for such individual services. Among this class of people, typical rentiers such as retired entrepreneurs, their widows and children, count less and less: with an increasing degree of industrialization new categories enter this class, for instance the growing groups of well-off professional people such as artists and journalists. In these cases, it is a matter of hardworking people who cannot spare the necessary time to deal with investment activities in the way they should. Big banks can never offer the kind of service their situation requires, at least not in the same way that private bankers are able to do.

Besides, the private bankers still retain some importance in the credit sector.

The growing diversity of conditions and the dynamics of events have led to the appearance of some gaps in market services, because the credit transactions of the big banks always remain of a somewhat stereotyped character. It is a further function of the private banker to fill such gaps, for he benefits from one very decisive advantage, in comparison with big banks. He has the merit of dealing with things directly.

For some years now, the BfG has been trying to reinforce the position of private bankers, primarily for regulative reasons. In places like Hamburg, Frankfurt and Düsseldorf, it has gone into partnership with old and well-known private banks. Such private bankers have to rely on a big bank for technical banking reasons and the BfG offers a very good background. Such a service can only be performed by an outside firm, since only such an outsider can offer them a guarantee that they will not ultimately be taken over. In the twenties this task was performed to some extent by the state-owned "Reichs-Kredit-Gesellschaft" (Credit Society of the Reich), which was the fourth of the five big Berlin Banks, smaller than the "Deutsche Bank", the "Dresdner Bank" and the "Commerz-Bank" but larger than the "Berlin Handelsgesellschaft". As a state bank without affiliated institutions, it already functioned as a clearing bank for private and provincial bankers and took charge of their Berlin clearings.

COLLABORATION WITH SAVINGS BANKS

Apart from cooperation with other banks owned by trade unions or cooperatives and its new activities with private bankers, the BfG also maintains close contacts with the clearing banks, the big money-collecting centres of the German savings banks network (112). This collaboration has been institutionalized through a joint partnership of several clearing banks with the "Bank für Gemeinwirtschaft" in the "Investitions – und Handelsbank" (Investment and Commerce Bank) at Frankfurt. There are three reasons for such collaboration between the BfG and the savings banks, one of a purely banking character, one related to commonweal principles and one to do with new tasks.

The banking reason for such collaboration can be seen in the fact that the savings banks traditionally have a large excess of liquidity. They are the large money-collecting centres in the economy.

The BfG on the other hand is a type of bank and has long been a bank with a surplus of good credits. The clearing banks and the BfG complement each other in business matters. It is also the case that the savings banks are traditionally bound to their localities by reason of their history and of their close bonds with the local set-up, while the BfG is a supra-regional business bank; it is often able to do business where savings banks are not active.

The second reason underlying the beneficial collaboration between clearing banks and the BfG is to be found in their common aims. Savings banks are the banks of municipalities and their associations. Their objectives are of a commonweal character, in the same way as those of the BfG, the trade union bank and the workers' movement in general. From this fact, very close contacts arise in almost all respects. Shared commonweal ambitions lead to the result that both groups of institutions very often find the same answers to the same questions, a fact which results almost automatically in close cooperation.

The third reason for useful cooperation between the BfG and the savings banks is to be found in a combination of the above two reasons especially with regard to infrastructure. Big projects designed to enlarge the infrastructure are, in most cases, of a new character. There is a vast field for collaboration in this sphere.

COMMONWEAL TASKS OF THE BfG

The commonweal tasks of the BfG may be summed up under the following three headings.

First of all, the bank has to maintain a high degree of liquidity for the trade unions' sake. Secondly, it has to safeguard the liquidity of other commonweal enterprises, and thirdly for regulative reasons it has the duty from time to time, of becoming actively engaged in the money and credit sector.

For the trade unions a high degree of liquidity at a moment's notice is an essential condition. Very soon, therefore, the question arose of how it would be possible for their funds to yield as high a rate of interest as possible, while at the same time remaining at the disposal of the unions whenever they were needed. For such a purpose the best method consists in having their own banking institutions. This secures both continous liquidity of capital and freedom of action for the unions.

This function of the bank is at the same time a real task in the commonweal sense. Trade unions are essential institutions of modern democratic industrial states. It arises from their tasks and their working methods that their solvency, at any moment, is an essential condition for their viability.

This is a social task of the bank, which in no way contradicts its entrepreneurial responsibility of operating as a universal bank for everybody. It will indeed have to do business with enterprises whose position is on the other side of the political arena, for it is part of the essence of a universal bank to remain accessible to all economic groups without distinction or reservation.

The second function of the bank is to secure the liquidity of the commonweal sector. This guarantee of security is by no means self-evident. The majority of commonweal enterprises have a different asset composition compared to private enterprise. As a result they cannot obtain equity in the same way as private enterprise does.

In an economic system that is becoming more and more capital-intensive, the mobilization of funds becomes an ever recurring necessity, so that the BfG gains an increasing importance by providing the financial basis of commonweal enterprises.

The bank has given an example by acquiring a shareholding of 25 % in the Wholesale Society of German Consumers' Cooperatives (GEG). It acquired this share in 1964. The other shares in the society (GEG) are held by consumers' cooperatives and by the GEG Pension Fund ("GEG–Rentenzuschusskasse"). Early in 1966, the GEG sold its BfG shares to the German trade unions, the other shareholder. Up to that date the consumers' cooperatives had held about 25% of the BfG's share capital. Through this double transaction the GEG obtained a considerable amount of additional owner's equity.

With the help of the BfG a further source of finance was opened up to consumers' cooperatives: the co-op real estate funds ("Co-op Immobilienfonds"). They were created with the assistance of the BfG, and their certificates are offered to the public through subsidiaries and agencies of BfG.

This change in partnership relations and the take-over of shares in commonweal enterprises through the BfG was, in fact, a once-for-all operation, with new issues on the capital market, which can occur whenever the firm's growth renders such operations necessary, provided its level of profitability is good enough to permit them to be carried out. It demonstrates quite clearly, however, how important close collaboration with a powerful bank is, just for normal rationalisation and growth processes in commonweal enterprises. Even if new ways of mobilizing capital are found for consumers' cooperatives and for other commonweal enterprises, close collaboration with a big bank nevertheless remains an indispensable condition. In such cases again, the only bank which will be able to help, is one that is not exclusively a "house bank", but works primarily and without reservation as a general business bank.

THE BfG'S REGULATIVE FUNCTION

The third commonweal task consists in what may be called the "regulative function" of BfG. Its function in regulating prices in the area of small loans is already well-known. Shortly after the currency reform (1948), commonweal banks concentrated intensively on instalment credits. The bank was able to help in this area, which was at the time the usual method of financing consumption needs by lower income groups and enabled them to re-equip their households. Later, it was particularly active in the small credits' sector offering clear and honest conditions.

The BfG also demonstrated its commonweal attitude in fostering house construction, primarily by means of bridging finance. In the "Neue Heimat", the bank has important business partners both on the commonweal side in the public utility housing societies and in a large number of private firms. For long-term business, the bank acquired an interlocking partnership in the "Braunschweig-Hannoversche Hypothekenbank" as well as the majority holding in the newly founded "Allgemeine Hypothekenbank A.G.", Frankfurt – two mortgage companies.

Furthermore, the BfG attempted to persuade workers to open bank accounts. It tried to develop new forms of savings bonds, adapted to the requirements of small savers. In the early sixties, as more and more firms began to pay wages and salaries by cheque, the BfG tried to introduce the "purchasing cheque", a cheque with a high guarantee of being honoured. The aim was to relieve customers of the need for frequent visits to their bank. This proposal could not be carried out, because the Federal Bank vetoed it. Early in 1966 the cheque card was introduced into the German banking system, and the idea of the purchasing cheque was thus realized in another way.

The new savings arrangements and the new forms of bond offered by the bank filled a gap in investment outlets, which had existed so far. Small savers invested their money primarily in fixed-term savings deposits. Though it is always possible to be repaid at short notice, experience shows that these accounts have a high degree of stability.

From their long-term savings, savers had not been getting any corresponding advantages in the form of higher yields or even additional payments. In the autumn of 1966 and in December 1968, BfG started two new forms of saving in order to find a solution to this problem: first of all, a ten-year savings bond subject to amortization, and secondly a new form of savings deposit, the "capital savings deposit", for a period of five years. Capital savings deposits cover round sums and are sold against once-for-all payments. Both forms of saving benefit from increasing rates of interest, the longer they are maintained. The savings bond of the BfG became a model for a new type of federal treasury bill in Germany. From this we see that the bank instituted new developments in the money and credit markets of this country.

One of the foremost tasks of a bank consists in the conversion of debts and in the financial restructuring of entire enterprises, without jeopardizing confidence in the firms and in economic activities in general. The BfG successfully carried out such a transaction in the case of the liquidation of both STINNES trusts. It did so, last but not least, in order to safeguard the interests of the trust's personnel, and by its action the bank fulfilled two very important commonweal tasks. First of all, it prevented the outbreak of a general crisis of confidence, by maintaining important enterprises, which were quite healthy in themselves to the benefit of the German economy, and by safeguarding the jobs of their staff. At the same time, it furnished unequivocal proof that commonweal behaviour and desires for profit need not conflict.

The fact that the BfG protects the public interest, is also manifest in its business cycle policy. During the recession of 1967, the bank continued to carry out an expansive credit policy in order to maintain business investment intentions.

Within its sphere of action and possibilities it helped to counteract the recession by means of such a policy. We might sum up the commonweal tasks of the BfG in the following way by formulating a "slogan": as a "house bank" of the trade unions and commonweal enterprises, it safeguards liquidity in this sector by acting as an intermediary in money flows among its members, enterprises and money and capital markets.

The BfG creates for trade unions the conditions for freedom of action. By its very existence the bank prevents a possible boycott of commonweal enterprises. Moreover, it still fulfils general tasks in the sphere of money and credit, by fostering competition in these areas and setting positive examples. The more the bank grows the more it will have to fulfil new tasks.

PART III

Outlines of a Theory of Commonweal Enterprise

Chapter 13

PLURALISM OF MOTIVES AND OBJECTIVES OF ENTERPRISE

We have so far described the origin of the idea of commonweal enterprise and the working methods of four groups of enterprises in this category. Our considerations now lead us to an outline of a general theory of commonweal enterprise. Considering that a definitive modern theory of what we call "commonweal enterprise" is still in the making, only the outlines of such a new theory can be offered in this context.

In doing so it must not be forgotten that the aims and motivations pursued by different economic agents, e.g. enterprises and households, have never been the same. To a large extent they have always been historically determined and preconceived. Whoever thinks that there have ever been aims and motives of secular validity over-looks the fact that all historical phenomena depend on particular circumstances of time and place. Man can only exist provided he can rely on satisfactory social conditions and institutions and create an order of things for himself which he has not received from nature (113).

At the same time the social and institutional framework of his existence is of a very different sort. Here we find mankind's dream of liberty: here man is making history, even if he is not always conscious of this.

From time to time the great variety of human possibilities will confront us more distinctly than before. Better and more detailed information about other nations and cultures will dissolve the geographic and historic conception of the world centred on Europe. All phenomena, including European, are to be seen within their framework of time and space and this will become still clearer, as horizons widen.

Alternative solutions elsewhere will demonstrate that there are a variety of possibilities for the form of social and institutional framework of human activity.

FOUR MODELS OF INDUSTRIALIZATION

It is in comparing the different processes of industrialization, that there is clearly recognized the breadth of action that exists with regard to industrialization, the most important social process of the last 200 years. The European-American pattern of industrialization is to be distinguished very clearly from similar completed processes, which have taken place autonomously in Japan and Russia. In Japan, industrialization took place after 1865 and in spite of similarity of technique there was a quite different institutional and social framework. Industrialization in the Soviet Union started under conditions which were diametrically opposed to those of the industrialization phases of Europe and Japan. The industrialization of China, the fourth model of industrialization, is at present proceeding on a largely autonomous basis. The large number of developing countries at the outset of industrialization leads to the expectation that there will be many more types of industrialization within the next few years than ever before.

Decades ago, Max Weber showed that European industrialization was the result of a unique historical combination of spiritual and social forces (114). This combination furnished at the time the prerequisite for a "chain reaction" of industrialization in Europe. Once the discovery of industrialization had taken place, other industrializations no longer required the combinations of forces existing in those days. What had once been historically necessary, is no longer logically necessary.

European industrialization took place in the 17th, 18th and 19th centuries, through private and commonweal enterprises. Both forms of enterprise took shape at the same time. Industrialization through private enterprises succeeded mercantilism, i.e. a system trying to develop the economy by means of state enterprise. The absolutist states, which were still relatively young, and the independent city states had already become active in the economic sphere before the beginning of industrialization proper. These states had carried on their own economic and customs policy in the 17th century by founding enterprises and fostering semi-private business foundations. This did not, however, lead to real industrialization. Their economic policies aimed solely at satisfying the desires for power and luxury of the respective oligarchies and dynasties. This class was very small and so the markets remained extremely small. There were no possibilities for economic expansion. In the 17th and 18th centuries mercantilist states had not yet actively engaged in such economic fields, as were liable to produce a great development of all productive forces.

THE BOURGEOIS MODEL OF INDUSTRIALIZATION

At that time in Europe the bourgeoisie alone was in a position to carry out industrialization through a combination of the desire for personal gain and modern rationalism. Consequently the process of industrialization in Europe and America was effected by profit inspired private enterprise, developed for the purpose by the bourgeoisie. The means of realizing this aim lay in applying rational, profit-maximizing calculations to investment in different markets (115). The bourgeoisie required of the state that it pass the laws necessary to ensure the efficacy of this type of enterprise, namely free market conditions rather than a corporative or state monopoly, and the free migration of people to wherever the best employment conditions could be obtained. By abolishing serfdom, the bourgeoisie forced the state to free labour and to introduce freedom of contract to economic activities. The bourgeoisie required further of the state that it create a rational and predictable system of law. And finally, also an important factor, it brought about the use of shares as claims to property.

During the nineteenth century, there were well-founded reasons for industrialization being based predominantly on private enterprise, and for the failure of alternative proposals presupposing other stimuli and forms of organization. An alternative form of enterprise to private business and its pursuit of profit did not contain the same degree of rationality. It was not seen clearly enough that the simple mobilization of labour was not sufficient for the making of a successful enterprise, and that success in business life nearly always implied a higher degree of capital intensity than before. People were not yet conscious of the fact that it is sometimes more important for a business firm to organize its financial basis correctly than to use its labour force in an optimal manner. During the 19th century there was a shortage of capital and an abundance of labour. This was of considerable consequence for the relative importance attributed to each factor and for the choice of business form. Finally, there was still a political argument: private entrepreneurs oriented towards profit, could look back on such spectacular success during the first stage of industrialization that a lasting need for non-capitalist forms of organization and enterprise was only felt to any degree rather late, and only in the case of certain social groups.

These spectacular achievements of primarily profit-oriented capitalist enterprise during the first stages of industrialization in Europe and in the United States had considerable repercussions for some time afterwards.

Even today, groups that by no means hold any vested interests in the matter still believe the private capitalist régime to be the best possible system for all times. People are convinced that it is only possible to do business in a rational way if businessmen pursue exclusively the aim of personal profit. Any other motivation or aim in economic life is considered to be less rational.

Thus, occurrences that are unique to certain historical periods are declared everlasting and absolute, and this blocks the way to new departures and possibilities.

It also reacts negatively upon the efficiency of the European system.

It entails a one-sided view and leads to the further consequence that the public authorities do not act with sufficient entrepreneurial spirit in those areas that are manifestly ill-suited to private forms of enterprise. Again, it follows that important forces find no possibility of pursuing other aims, or of acting in a way that differs from the traditional motivation of business life.

THE PRINCIPLE OF RATIONALITY AND THE IDEA OF ECONOMIC EFFICIENCY

If a unique historical situation is attributed with absolute values, then the profit motive, and with it capitalism, are similarly regarded (116). This stems from an implicit but enduring false identification of efficiency with the profit motive. In this way it is ignored that economic efficiency represents only one form of the principle of rationality, in which the profit motive is applied to the search for economic efficiency in the particular aspect of the rational use of a firm's capital (117). Walter Eucken has made some noteworthy contributions to this complex of questions (118). He thinks that ignorance of "economic principles", just as ignorance of history or perhaps both together, has led to the impression that man would act with economic rationality only during the so-called "capitalist epoch". It is also believed that other principles prevailed in former epochs and in other civilizations. Eucken says of this: "There is not a shadow of proof for such a theory, if one looks back on history" (119).

Men have always subjectively followed the principle of economic rationality, though in an objective sense they may often be considered to have contravened it. "In all times and places men seek their economic calculations and actions to attain a particular end with the least possible consumption of resources" (120). According to Eucken this principle of economic rationality is then a general principle inspiring all intelligent human action, and it should not be confounded with capitalist principles. "Planning and acting on the basis of economic rationality is not limited to being a peculiarity of the 'trader' or even of the trader in modern European or American times. It is a principle inspiring all intelligent action, in general" (121).

According to Eucken, therefore, the principle of economic rationality constitutes a constant element in human society. In historical reality, however, it appears under many different forms. In order to make this evident, Eucken sets out four pairs of antitheses, within whose framework all economic activity takes place. According to him they suffice to describe reality (122). First of all, man only acts subjectively according to the principle of economic rationality; objectively, he may very well contravene it. Secondly, man has either constant or variable needs. Thirdly, he wants either the highest possible net income or as good a subsistence level as possible. Fourthly, he either plans for the long run or the short run. Fifthly, he behaves either traditionally or rationally.

Eucken illustrates this system of antitheses in comparing an American entrepreneur A and a French peasant R. "A acts objectively according to the principle of economic rationality (1), has a variable range of unlimited needs (2), follows the principle of highest possible net income (3), prepares extensive economic plans (4) and is, besides, not very deeply rooted in traditional obligations (5). R., the French peasant, follows the principle of economic rationality only in a subjective manner (1), has a constant level of needs (2), but satisfies these needs as far as possible according to the principle of the highest possible net income (3), provides at the same time – though in a different way and with fewer risks – for the more distant future (4), and is, moreover, strongly influenced by imponderables" (123).

PLURALISM OF GOALS

Not only does the principle of economic rationality appear in various forms, but it may also be used for numerous purposes. There is no attitude in life that by itself corresponds to the principle of economic rationality; the range of the latter must always be considered within the context of concrete goals. It strives only at rationality of behaviour, and this behaviour may be quite different in realization under outwardly similar conditions: it all depends on the fundamental aims, with what sort of temperament and willpower the objective is pursued, and how the rejected objects and objectives are discarded (124). The application of the principle of economic rationality does not depend on the principle of profitability. "It is possible to act in an economically rational manner even where the services produced are provided free" (125) – provided that such behaviour is prescribed for the enterprise in question.

Whoever declares the pursuit of profit to be the only goal of economic activity confuses ends and means. This is logically quite evident and can be proved from history. Participants in economic life almost never aimed at profits as their sole or even primary purpose. Profits were not the real purpose; they were merely a means to realize other social or existential aims. Private entrepreneurs in reality always pursued other goals. This can be seen from the biographies of individual enterprises. Businessmen pursued quite a collection of personal aims: self-assurance, pleasure in work and achievements, social recognition, improvement in social status and a secure position in society.

When it came to profits, they almost never aimed at the highest profit possible but only at customary levels of profits. Hardly ever was there a desire for the highest standard of living imaginable but rather for that which was appropriate under the particular conditions. There were always norms limiting wealth and luxury. The absolute pursuit of profit was even frowned upon in most societies. Whoever aspired after profits alone always ran the risk of becoming a social outcast.

In every mixed society there is a pluralism of motives in action, and this pluralism finds its expression in different combinations of aims as professed by individual business units. There are the entrepreneurs in pursuit of profit and primarily following private interests, whose highest goal is not a social task and for whom production only constitutes a means to an end. But alongside such people, there were always others, who in their activities served the common good, their all-embracing aim consisting in the fulfilment of well-defined tasks or services and for whom the realization of profits was only a means of realizing certain aims. Pluralism of aims always found its expression in a plurality of types of enterprises (126).

In economic reality vast differences are to be found between enterprises. "According to the character of owners (members) and their goals, we may distinguish various types of business units: private capitalist, State capitalist, 'free' commonweal and public enterprises, of which the latter may either be purely public or of mixed enterprise" (127).

Amongst private enterprises can be mentioned commercial firms aiming at profit maximization and which are working primarily for higher returns; they have to be distinguished from corporative enterprises following the principle of professional activity.

In the latter case the independent exercise of professional skills will be in the forefront. Both principles, the business principle as well as the professional principle, appear in contrast to a third one, the service principle which is followed by public enterprise.

"Between these two limiting cases of entrepreneurial activities, there are the fully capitalist enterprises, whose owners feel more or less strong affinities towards the respective branch, the inherited enterprise or both. And there are the constrained capitalist enterprises, in which apart from the goals of the owners, the goals of other people in the enterprise (paid managers and personnel) are also relevant. If, in such enterprises, the business aims of the owners conflict with aims pursued by other groups, the owners may nevertheless be free of constraints in that they feel bound to the particular firm or enterprise by professional ties or similar grounds such as tradition or inclination. Links of this kind can certainly endure" (128).

And, last but not least, autonomous and purely profit maximizing enterprises under a single owner will not follow one unique goal as a rule, but rather an entire collection of targets. Such a range of aims may consist of goals "partly compatible with or complementary to each other, partly opposing each other; in the latter case there will be the need to reconcile them" (129). Thus, for instance, the aim of profitability almost always conflicts with security, independence with unification, and precaution with growth. For all these aims there is no common denominator of success!

Chapter 14

THE NOTION OF COMMONWEAL ENTERPRISE

There is a widespread opinion that only if the search for private profit is the central motive of entrepreneurs will it be possible to succeed in business. That opinion must be refuted. In real life there is a vast multitude of business enterprises pursuing quite different aims. For the question under consideration, the decisive criterion concerns the objectives pursued by business firms. It is at the same time the fundamental criterion for distinguishing one enterprise from another within the framework of what is called "the morphology of enterprises".

First of all, the distinction must be drawn between private enterprise and commonweal enterprise. In this sense, "private enterprises" are defined as such firms as serve primarily the interests of their owners; this becomes quite clear if we realize that their profits accrue to private individuals. Such private firms only pursue the public interest as a secondary objective. By "commonweal enterprises", however, are understood firms that are primarily dedicated to the public interest, to the common good, or "common weal". This becomes clear in so far as their profits are allocated to purposes serving the common interests of society.

This distinction between private and commonweal enterprise is no question of legal form or ownership. On the contrary, this distinction aims at a classification based on the inner character-forming forces and on the external organizational form. The private versus commonweal classification is a classification according to the nature of the enterprise (130). The private or public use of profit, at any given time, is, therefore, an important distinguishing characteristic.

COMMONWEAL ENTERPRISE

As regards the definition of the concept "commonweal enterprise", I prefer to follow Gerhard Weisser. His definition corresponds to the terms chosen by the Scientific Council of the "Gesellschaft für öffentliche Wirtschaft und Gemeinwirtschaft" ("Society for Public and Commonweal Economy", Berlin), and runs as follows: "Commonweal enterprises are individual business units, whose profits, and on occasions even the production itself, are dedicated, in accordance with the purposes for which it was created, directly to the welfare of a superior body, or to the development of an idea which this body regards as a mandatory objective. The enterprise should, moreover, have an institutional form appropriate to the goal to which it is devoted" (131).

This definition denotes a "real type" in the terminology of Walter Eucken. This means that, in real life, there will never be a pure type of commonweal enterprise. Such a pure type could only be developed through an "abstraction emphasizing certain points". Commonweal enterprises will, therefore, never be able to embody certain qualities (which will now be dealt with in detail) in a pure sense, but only to a greater of lesser extent.

1. Commonweal enterprises refer to individual business units, i.e. to enterprises in the widest sense of the word, and, therefore, to enterprises resembling institutions or even administrative set-ups.

2. The end result of commonweal enterprises, at times through their profits, at times by their very actions, is to promote the public interest or the common good.

3. The statement "in accordance with the purposes for which it was created" implies that this does not happen indirectly, or "nolens volens", through the pressure of the market mechanism. The same statement implies that the common or public interest will be appreciated for its own inherent value and will be sought for its own sake.

4. It is not possible with regard to commonweal enterprises to reduce the general aim "common good" or "common weal" to more detailed objectives. In the following text, however, a further examination will be made of the two concepts, "common good" and "public interest". At this juncture, however, we do not enter into a more detailed exposition.

5. If we talk of an "institutional form appropriate to the goal, to which it is devoted", this means that the commonweal enterprise has to be constituted and institutionalized as such. It is distinguished from private enterprises by the institutionalization of the basic commonweal principles that inspire it, even when private enterprises exercise temporarily certain commonweal functions for charity or as patrons of literature or arts. The institutional form need not be fixed in the legal sense. For instance, real security in the fulfilment of this function may be achieved through a certain sociological composition of the directors of the enterprise, and this will suffice to determine the essential traits of the enterprise's character.

If we look at an enterprise of this category from the outside, it will more or less resemble a private profit-motivated enterprise. To recapitulate, we may say that it can be distinguished from private enterprises "only" through its aims and the motivation of its activities – in other words, only through its inner drives. These aims represent the direct realization of the public interest or of the "common good" or "commonweal" in two ways, alternative or additive.

1. First of all, it does so by setting aside for certain purposes the proceeds of its activities, i.e. its profits. "Profits" in this context do not mean the usual return on capital on the market – this, in our terminology, would be "capital cost". On the contrary we are talking here of genuine "surplus".

2. Secondly, it should be stated that commonweal enterprise pursues its aims by undertaking certain (additional) activities, on behalf of the whole community and in the common interest.

3. The determining of aims cannot be left to the whims of individuals or of a certain group. It must be established on an institutionalized level.

The decisive element for a commonweal enterprise lies in the fact that it seeks to promote the common good as a direct consequence of the aims it is itself pursuing. It also does not matter which motives the managers may have in carrying out individual activities of their enterprise. Such motives do not form part of a definition of the goals of this enterprise. The real *raison d'être* of the business unit concerned can only derive from the intentions of its founders and owners, and from the general context of social relationships that constitute the atmosphere surrounding that particular enterprise (132).

THE *raison d'être* OF THE ENTERPRISE CONCERNED

As a complement to the definition so far developed two concepts remain to be examined: that of the underlying *raison d'être* of the enterprise concerned, and that of the "common good" or "common weal".

Among the established and real *raisons d'être* which distinguish the enterprise, apart from numerous more formal criteria, is included a number of direct or derived interests and obligations, which determine the existence of the enterprise, its current behaviour or that of its responsible officials (133). "The *raison d'être* results from the intention of its founders and owners, and (or) from the general environment of social conditions for that particular enterprise" (134).

Now, the *raison d'être* cannot be thought of as embodying something inexorably fixed, no matter whether an "objectively fixed aim" is to be understood as a metaphysical category or as an idea constituting part of a given platonic or Hegelian "constellation of ideas".

The *raison d'être*, we are talking of, cannot be derived either as an objective fact, from the actual shape or transformation of productive conditions. "It is not possible to derive aims from declarations about things that exist or are developing historically . . . There must always be a decision on top of that . . . ." (135).

Various attempts to provide a *raison d'être* for different enterprises are themselves based on certain fundamental motives of action, which cannot be traced to any remoter sources. These basic motives are themselves the final objective that one wants to realize, or to reject for its own sake. In this context, it does not matter whether the contents of these basic motives, which always have a psychological tinge, are to be considered as eternally and generally valid, or whether they are only valid for certain people at certain times; all this is irrelevant to the question of the *raison d'être* of enterprises. It does not matter either, whether and how far those who profess these fundamental aims are really fully conscious of the immediate urges, interests or obligations, out of which these fundamental motives arise.

The basic motives have an effect on the *raison d'être* of the enterprise concerned, determining in this way the type and behaviour of the firm. For instance, an entrepreneur who is subject to some religious or humanitarian convictions will strive to bring about a good relationship towards his work people for its own sake, and not only to further an increase in his profits. This does not preclude the possibility that he will simultaneously welcome the rise in productivity brought about by a good business climate inside his firm and take it into account in his plans. It would be a gross simplification to reduce each and every humanitarian attitude to profit considerations; in doing so, one would also unduly exaggerate the importance of the profit motive.

THE CONCEPT OF "COMMON GOOD" OR "COMMON WEAL"

It is the *raison d'être* of commonweal enterprise to aim at the common good or common interest. The concept of a "commonweal enterprise", therefore, is itself based upon the underlying concept of the common good.

Taken by itself, however, and isolated from the conditions under which the term is used, the concept "common good" constitutes nothing but an empty formula. By an "empty box" we wish to convey the idea of an empty structure, which can be filled with all sorts of contents of a most contradictory character. Similar words serving to convey the same idea are also merely "empty boxes" – e.g. terms such as "public or general interest", "public utility", "Welfare maximum" etc. The same holds true of various related terms as, for instance, "Daseinsfürsorge" (provident activities to improve living conditions), "the principle of solidarity" etc. In mediaeval times, the question of the common good was called the question of the "bonum commune".

Very frequently in the field of politics we encounter terms and statements devoid of any contents. In this area such terms provide compromise solutions. Forces, whose interests or values conflict in reality, can find temporary agreement in statements or concepts, which can be filled with contradictory views.

Nevertheless, there is no "empty box" that is so empty that it cannot at least be negatively defined. If we apply this consideration to the term "common good", it means that the concept "common weal" always applies to aims diametrically opposed to egotism both of individuals as well as of groups. What, therefore, can be said with some certainty about the term "common good" is that it always aims at the welfare of a community, however we may define such a community, and whatever may be understood by the common good or welfare of that community.

IDEALISTIC AND RATIONALISTIC METHODS

In the search for the common good, two methods are applied to solve the problem. Neither of them reaches a satisfactory solution, but practically all existing social concepts today are based upon one or other of these ideas. They are called the "idealistic" and "rationalistic" methods of establishing the will of the society or the common good (136).

The idealistic method of finding the will of the community or people is based upon the consideration that it is somehow possible for human reasoning and thought to discover the "bonum commune". Practically all dictatorial and paternalistic institutions are models on the way to idealistic recognition of the common good.

In all such institutions the "well-understood interests" of all people, of the nation, of mankind etc. will be determined by an individual or group very often quite independently of the real interests and desires of many citizens and consumers. We must not only emphasize that such a system contains quite inexhaustible possibilities of abuse; it does not solve these problems either, but only serves to personalize them. It determines who will say what the common good is, and what the will of the people should be.

The rationalistic method is almost as unsatisfactory. Instead of human beings, it charges a mechanism with the task of determining the contents of the "common weal". In the course of history quite a number of rationalistic mechanisms have been devised to determine these contents. They all have one feature in common; that instead of the sovereignty of the "strong man", a sort of people's or consumers' sovereignty is postulated, from which the will of the community, the *volonté générale,* is to be derived, for instance in the form of a demand function, after the innumerable individual desires have been collected and filtered, as it were.

Among the various mechanisms that we may apply for this purpose, two categories may be distinguished, namely the system of "direct democracy" and that of "representative democracy". Under the first term the direct transmission of the people's will, we include the Soviet (or council) system, many systems of joint (or workers') control and the free market economy. To the second category, that of the indirect or representative systems, belong the cooperative system, the corporative State or the system of upper and lower houses and chambers, and modern parliamentary democracy. In these systems, politicians or entrepreneurs have acted correctly in the economic or political sphere, if they succeed in obtaining the largest number of votes or the highest sales figure.

Idealistic as well as rationalistic attempts to develop universally valid concepts of the "common good" are based upon the desire to bring about harmony and they all aim at or originate from the notion of a "sound world". In doing so, they very often served as pretexts for authoritarian practices and inability to make decisions. Both tendencies – power politics and inactivity – often disguise themselves behind nebulous ideas of the "common good". Conservative elements are very often inclined to counteract claims for social change with the harmony argument and so avoid the social problem. But revolutionary forces also employ nebulous ideas of general harmony to at least the same extent. They flee from the hard facts of reality into a dream world of harmony (137).

In reality, idealistic and rationalistic systems intermingle when determining the contents of the concept of the "common good". In the Socialist systems of the Eastern Block, consumption is regulated by planning, but planners have to take increasing account of the wishes of consumers. A system, therefore, that is theoretically based upon idealistic concepts, will be increasingly complemented by rationalistic elements in determining its contents.

In contrast to the countries of the Eastern Block our systems are essentially rationalistic. There is not a single political group in the West that believes that the "common good" should be determined by a small group of people. Nevertheless, groups professing different programmes of economic policy never completely ignore the necessity of correcting consumers' wishes by legal measures and by means of modern publicity or advertising methods.

In any system consumers' desires have to be influenced in some way, because many consumers do not know what is really good for them.

To a certain extent, however, we must distinguish between real interests and what may be termed "well-understood interests" of individuals, denoting by the latter term those interests an individual would defend were he sufficiently informed. This distinction is feasible to a certain extent, and is accepted in many cases, e.g. it applies to obligatory schooling, inoculation, prohibition of the narcotics trade etc. Politicians are already obliged for purely technical reasons to adopt an idealistic attitude, for they have to dictate certain things in a paternalistic manner, because it is not possible to refer in each and every situation to the interests, preferences or decisions of individual citizens or consumers. In doing so, they have to derive their decisions from political norms, which in turn, will be partly based upon the value judgements of citizens or consumers, and partly on those of politicians or entrepreneurs. Any political activity or act of economic policy always means that certain advantages and disadvantages will be conferred by forcible methods in the well-understood (though unconscious) interests of the citizen, the action being based on norms, political or otherwise, and on the gounds of the declared contents of the common good.

THE BASIC ELEMENTS WHICH DETERMINE CONTENTS: VALUES

In spite of all mechanisms allowing for self-determination on the part of citizens or consumers, there must nevertheless be some amount of government activity.

The decisions of politicians in power must be derived from political norms, and these norms, in turn, must be based partly on value judgments, which cannot be traced to any deeper sources, and about which, consequently, there can be no further rational argument. Value judgments can only be made explicit and it will be left to the sound judgment of other people whether they adopt or reject them.

Again, it must not be forgotten that the concepts of "common good" or "common weal" may take on varying aspects. This does not only hold true of differences of opinion between upper and lower classes, age groups, politicians and citizens, entrepreneurs and consumers, town and countryside. For centuries, people have been looking for the "bonum commune", the "common weal", valid for each and everyone, and for the public interest. This search had been basically in vain, because none of these ideas is equally valid and, therefore, applicable to each and every person. It is not possible, in any historical situation, to pass judgment – in a way that may be verifiable – upon the contents of the concept of "common good" or "public interest". Especially in pluralistic societies such as ours today, there are very many different ideas and images of what is human welfare and human happiness. We are almost tempted to say that this must be so, by definition! In pluralistic societies, there are even public utility objectives, which contradict each other, and there are concepts of the public interest that mutually exclude each other.

For instance, it is quite possible at one time and under the same conditions, for large groups of the population to support certain ideas reminiscent of the corporative State, while other groups follow democratic ideals. If this is the case, the former group will imagine that a sound peasantry and a strong middle-class constitute the foundation of state and society, and they will see the greatest degree of welfare in high prices, which are to the advantage of producers. On the contrary, the other group will look for the "common weal" in the greatest happiness of the greatest number of people, and they will confirm that the public interest is best supported when buying prices are low, and producers' prices are consequently also as low as possible.

Today, it is possible to find realistic definitions of what the "common good" ought to be, definitions that are free of any mistakes, whether conservative or revolutionary, and which do not envisage a "sound world", and do not aim at a harmonically ordered society. It must be accepted that there are social conflicts, and that the notion of the "common good" or "common weal" must be taken for what it is, namely a cipher to be filled with real and meaningful contents, by means of proposals made by competing social forces. All political conflicts ultimately derive from certain conceptions of the "common good" and social forces, using different concepts of what the "common weal" is to be, and which compete to win favour with the general public.

NO RELATIVISM CONCERNING THE "COMMON GOOD"

We do not want to defend any empty relativism. There are two limits to useful definitions of the concept of the "common good" or "common weal". The first limit lies in the fact that every thought and wish is time-bound. This means that no concept of the "common good" can be evolved without reference to a concrete historical environment. For instance, it is today no longer possible to propose the idea of a cooperative state. Such an idea belongs to the past. The same is true of the council concept – the idea of the "Soviet" State. Ideas regarding the "common good" can only be presented within the framework of political, scientific and social debates, which have taken place within the last few decades.

There is still a second restriction on the freedom of choice of ideas concerning the "common good". This requires that such ideas, if they are to be taken seriously, must satisfy the condition of helping to make the world more humane. Confronted with the tools of modern warfare, mankind can only survive if on this earth relations are made more civilised. It is no longer possible to harbour ideas of the "common good" which are inspired by nationalist feelings, racial discrimination or fascist concepts, given the terrible arsenal of weapons of annihilation. If they were ever to be realized again, they would lead to the self-destruction of mankind.

Within these two limits, of time and of humane considerations, manifold interpretations of the notion "common good" can, nevertheless, be adopted. They should actively compete for the approval of the public. The democratic process of approval or rejection, after due discussion about the contents of the notion "common good", will then decide in any specific situation, what society understands by the term "common good".

PLURALISM OF AIMS PURSUED BY ENTERPRISES

The idea of the "common good' as propounded in this context is based upon a realistic hypothesis, viz. the existence of variations in the concept of "common good", which are competing for the public's approval. Such concepts will be formulated in various ways: in party programmes, in declarations, and in practical work in the political, cultural or social spheres. One possible interpretation of the notion of the "common good" consists in the foundation and maintenance of commonweal enterprises. In this way the concept of "common good" as held by certain social groups, can, at a point in time, be given a concrete form for a well-defined purpose and can be canvassed before a wider public.

Commonweal enterprises, working in full knowledge of the existence of a pluralistic society, and taking all the conflicts arising within it for granted, will bring to the forefront all such social tensions and contradictions. In doing so, they help to bring about a dispassionate debate. They help to limit such conflicts to areas where they belong, and they prevent their extension into areas where they are inappropriate. The notion of the "common good" as we understand it, is, therefore, both realistic and useful. It would be advantageous in discussions on social policy, if all groups could state their conflicts more clearly and initiate a public debate on their ideas of the common good more frequently than hitherto and in a concrete manner, even in the field of commonweal enterprises. It would then be easier to confine such conflicts to the areas immediately concerned, and public debate as to the best way of realizing the common good would be made clearer.

Again, if the idea of the "common good" could be based upon pluralistic reality, a more tolerant attitude would ensue. Recognition of pluralism in the business sector leads to the result that even the champions of commonweal enterprise would no longer declare their ideal to be applicable to the entire society, as Walter Rathenau had been doing in the aftermath of the First World War (138).

If they declare commonweal principles to be applicable to all economic agents and to the whole of economic life, they are simply going from one extreme to another and are guilty of committing the same mistake, which occurs today because people exaggerate the importance of the motive of private gain. Any claim for the exclusiveness of a principle of conduct contradicts the great variety of structures in the world and the fact that there are many different motives at work. On the contrary, we see inestimable value in the great variety of types of enterprise in business life, from the point of view of creating as much freedom as possible.

Chapter 15

CATEGORIES, PROBLEMS AND TENDENCIES OF COMMONWEAL ENTERPRISES

As in the case of private enterprise businesses, there are many forms of commonweal enterprise. The multitude of types can be represented by contrasting certain terms by way of antithesis, for instance, the concepts of "private business" and "commonweal enterprise", and by combining them with another antithesis, production for profit and production for need, so as to get a first general idea. In this way four types of enterprise can be worked out, which as a first distinction can be of a certain didactic value.

	Private economy	Commonweal economy
Production for profit	capitalist enterprise	government enterprise
Production for need	mutual aid ("self-help") enterprise	supply enterprise

Private firms based on the profit motive represent the primary type of capitalist enterprise today. If such a firm is the property of the state, and if its receipts accrue to the state, we speak of a "government or state enterprise". Many self-help and mutual aid enterprises are directed towards both the satisfaction of needs and towards private advantage; this applies to a large proportion of commercial cooperatives. Public utilities are predominantly based upon the two principles of the satisfaction of basic needs and of commonweal economy.

FOUR GROUPS OF COMMONWEAL ENTERPRISES

In any case, the comparison of private business production and production for need is not very fruitful (139).

If we want to illustrate the concept of commonweal economy, we should examine the question of the aims that are pursued, combining this investigation with a classification of these enterprises according to their respective owners. This means that we should classify them as public enterprises, enterprises of the commonweal housing sector, cooperative enterprises, and finally "free" commonweal enterprises.

All enterprises, no matter whether their legal form is determined by private company law or by public law, owned by state authorities, viz. the Federal Government, "Land" Governments and municipalities or their associations, provided they are fulfilling public tasks, are part of the public sphere. This means that their aim should not be one of earning high revenues for the fiscal authorities. The most important and biggest enterprises of each country belong to the public sector, namely public banks, i.e. the central bank, a number of other state banks working for certain regions or sectors, numerous public mortgage establishments and the savings banks. Furthermore, public transport belongs to this sector: the railways, most urban transport systems, and in many cases also the air transport companies. The third big public area of activity is that of public communications, including the post office, and the broadcasting and the television corporations. The fourth group are the enterprises distributing gas, water and electricity. The fifth and final group is represented by public enterprise in the field of health, namely public hospitals, sanatoria and rehabilitation establishments.

In most cases, the commonweal purpose of public enterprise is guaranteed by the owner. In most cases also it is fixed by statute, and its details are defined by specially constituted administrative boards. The public interest is served here by the provision of services to particular groups of people in particular areas.

The second group of commonweal enterprises consists of public utility and commonweal housing societies, some the property of public authorities, some of free social associations.

There is no longer any controversy about their functions, namely to plan, to build and to run houses and entire towns as well as large areas of infrastructure. This rôle is steadily gaining in importance. What is more difficult is the classification of cooperatives as commonweal enterprises; this category comprises agricultural, industrial, commercial, credit and consumers' cooperatives. These enterprises are designed to further the economic activities or household interests of their members, and in doing so they are often directly motivated by commercial gain.

In principle, cooperatives cannot be considered a priori as enterprises of a commonweal character. Nevertheless, the majority of German cooperatives are indeed oriented towards commonweal aims, in so far as they help to bring about an improvement in living conditions for social groups, to whom the society owes certain well-defined obligations, and in so far as they perform social and political tasks (140). Furthermore, they are of a commonweal character, in so far as they exercise regulative functions (141).

The fourth group of commonweal enterprises consist of firms belonging to the sector of "free" commonweal economy. Here it is possible to distinguish between "free" commonweal enterprises of the German workers' movement and other "free" commonweal firms.

The Four Categories of Commonweal Economy

1. *Public enterprise – enterprises of the*
   (a) Federal Government,
   (b) "Land" Governments,
   (c) Municipalities,
   (d) Municipal associations and other local authorities.
2. *Commonweal housing enterprises*
   (a) Public utility housing societies,
   (b) Commonweal firms for town construction.
3. *Cooperative societies*
   (a) Agricultural (Raiffeisen),
   (b) Industrial and commercial (Schulze-Delitzsch),
   (c) Credit cooperatives,
   (d) Consumers' cooperatives.
4. *The "free" commonweal sector*
   (a) Commonweal enterprises of the German workers' movement,
   (b) Other commonweal enterprises of other associations.

DECISION-MAKING IN COMMONWEAL ENTERPRISES

If we classify commonweal enterprises by categories of owner, this is at the same time a classification by groups exercising influence on decision-making in the enterprises concerned. The aims pursued by the commonweal firms take on a more concrete form in the continuing exchange between the management and the boards of control, viz. its supervisory or administrative council. The management should always be composed of experts in that particular branch, while the supervisory or administrative council should consist of representatives of corporations and organizations owning the particular commonweal enterprise. Its composition will differ depending on its character, be it a public enterprise, a cooperative society or a "free" commonweal enterprise.

There are two factors that determine the way the supervisory organs of commonweal enterprises function and the direction they take. First of all, we have to consider the nature of the owner, whether it is a public or local authority, a cooperative society or an association pursuing certain interests. Secondly, we have to ask how its supervisory organ is composed, if its members belong to a homogeneous group, or whether persons of heterogeneous tendencies or interests are united in one and the same body. The disposition and capacity to take decisions in the enterprise concerned will be determined by the high or low degree of homogeneity or heterogeneity of the controlling group, while the first factor, the nature of the owner himself, will have a decisive influence on the contents of the concept "commonweal economy".

Commonweal enterprises owned by public authorities will interpret the term "commonweal" as the "common good" of the people in their particular territories. Public enterprises belonging to the Federal Government will see the "common good" in defending national interests, while other enterprises that are the property of "Land" governments or associations of municipalities and local authorities will consider the well-being of the people in their regions or municipalities.

At the same time certain political tinges will appear in such definitions. It will be discernible whether the municipality concerned is dominated for instance by a "bourgeois" group or by a group related to the working-class. In these cases the emphasis will then remain with the interests of the bourgeoisie or the working-class respectively.

In the case of "free" commonweal enterprises as well, the political and social preferences of the social groups, on which these enterprises are based, will enter the commonweal formula of these firms. If a "free" commonweal enterprise belongs to the workers' movement, it will represent a concept of "commonweal economy" based upon the needs of large groups of the population. It is, however, also possible for a new "free" commonweal enterprise to be dedicated to the advancement of science. In this case the fulfilment of the "common good" will be chiefly seen in scientific progress. Even an enterprise catering for sick or handicapped people may be of a commonweal type. In such cases the notion of "commonweal enterprise" will be interpreted in the sense of welfare activities or social assistance. Furthermore it is conceivable that a commonweal enterprise could dedicate itself to the development of aesthetic and artistic values.

For entrepreneurial functions the degree of homogeneity in management is important. This depends on the composition of the groups upon which the enterprise is based. If a commonweal enterprise is based upon large groups that are divided in themselves, conflicts will often appear within the leading group. For that reason there may be difficulties in defining concrete aims. Instead, there will arise vague formulations of the common good, and only such services will be rendered whose use to the community is beyond question. Heterogeneous groups will encounter difficulties in arriving at clear-cut decisions.

Entrepreneurial difficulties of public enterprise frequently result from the fact that public corporations have to pay attention to too many divergent tendencies. This will be particulary bad in enterprises whose centres of power contain representatives of many different pressure groups.

In this case the corporation will either do everything at the same time so as to satisfy everybody, or it will limit itself to certain measures that are obviously inevitable and so be constrained from doing anything new. The bigger and more heterogeneous the decision-making group, which formulates the aims of the enterprise, the less it will be an enterprise and the more a public authority.

By comparison commonweal enterprises of free social associations or groups are much more flexible from an entrepreneurial point of view. The groups standing behind them are more homogeneous. It is, therefore, easier for them to make decisions. The goal "common good" may be defined much more rapidly and concretely. "Free" commonweal enterprises need not limit themselves to activities that are obviously necessary. This is the advantage of "free" commonweal enterprises compared with public enterprises. Here we find the basic reason for their existence. They are able to operate more easily amidst a multiplicity of forces, and it is easier for them to introduce new commonweal points of view into economic life by applying entrepreneurial methods.

The size of commonweal enterprises also has a bearing on the concept of the "common good". Big commonweal enterprises are only possible if large organizations or local authorities stand behind them, and these organizations themselves are likely to be differentiated regionally or sociologically. This again protects the enterprises against any subservience to the interests of small minorities and against their becoming merely instruments of an association or an enterprise catering solely for its members. The structural characteristics, which depend on the size of such an enterprise, have, therefore, a certain bearing on the commonweal concept that is embodied.

CAPITAL AS A FACTOR OF PRODUCTION IN COMMONWEAL ENTERPRISES

The "common good" concept embodied in commonweal enterprise is further determined by the fact that modern industrial societies are developing more and more into "affluent societies".

In former times the economy was seen as consisting of a profit motivated sector and a sector dealing with production for need and the commonweal economy was largely interpreted as forming part of the latter sector. In this context the idea of production for basic needs presupposes the satisfying of basic needs, however these are to be defined. But in an economic system of growing affluence it becomes very difficult, apart from a few areas, to speak of well-defined needs. Every new pound or dollar injected into such an affluent society means that the consumer will be able to buy a new commodity, and his freedom to choose this or that commodity will be ever greater. Industrial societies produce more and more "superfluous" goods, and consumers accept them – goods, whose only function is to make life more beautiful. If we define commonweal economy as covering purely basic needs, we should limit it to basic activities, such as the supply of water, gas and electricity, and such a constraint would correspond neither to the actual situation nor to the necessities of our times.

For commonweal enterprises seen in the framework of a highly industrialized affluent society, capital assumes a new importance as a factor of production. Very few public services supply only basic goods to consumers; in most cases commonweal enterprises offer goods and services in competition with other firms, and as their customers are free to accept or reject them, these enterprises are quite justified in financing themselves through their prices. When they offer their goods and services on the market in competitive conditions their success on the market is a yardstick of their efficiency and shows whether the goals and the methods of the commonweal enterprise are accepted by the public. If a commonweal enterprise offers goods and services that are not absolute necessities, the return on capital will become as important to such an enterprise as it is for private business. The return on capital will help to secure not only its financial autonomy, as it does in the case of public utilities, but it will also justify its claim on this capital in the face of competitive demands. The analysis of investment projects has been developed in modern enterprise with a view to using available funds in the most profitable manner.

It is for this reason that people believed for several generations, that successful business could only be done under the motive of personal gain. Nowadays the analysis of investment projects is an entrepreneurial technique without ethical content, and it can be applied to every imaginable entrepreneurial purpose. The principle of the most profitable use of private capital has been transformed into the principle of economic efficiency in the use of capital as such, independently of the purpose for which the capital is used. The principle in this form remains valid for commonweal enterprises as well. Public enterprises are able to give up their antiquated system of accounting ("cameralism") and adopt commercial principles without giving up their objectives based on the principle of the "common good".

CONVERGENCE OF PRIVATE AND COMMONWEAL LARGE-SCALE ENTERPRISE

Commonweal enterprises must pay attention to their profit position. It is by no means "sinful", or an accident of the capitalist spirit of the fifties, that these enterprises should more and more adopt commercial methods. This is the consequence of increasing size and growing capital intensity of all modern enterprises. The bigger commonweal enterprises are and the greater their capital intensity, the less will public authorities and associations owning such enterprises be able and prepared to satisfy the enormous and growing capital requirements of such enterprises out of public funds. These corporations and companies will thus have to meet their capital requirements to a growing extent by competing with private firms on the open capital market. As their size and capital intensity increase these firms must, therefore, pay more and more attention to their profit and loss account.

In many cases in the past, large capital-intensive public enterprises did not follow the principle of simply meeting basic needs. The Prussian railways earned quite considerable profits for the Prussian State prior to the First World War. At the time, it was thought that this was quite in order, and nobody spoke of any contradiction between this and their commonweal tasks. Many public enterprises in the gas, water and electricity sectors found themselves in a similar situation.

One cannot help feeling that the theory according to which public enterprise should quote only cost price, was simply a consequence of the shortages of the twenties, thirties and forties. Finally, in the fifties, an attitude born out of necessity was transformed into an ideology to combat the economic activities of public enterprise. As a counterpart to the assimilation of the behaviour of public and commonweal enterprises to that of private big business, there is another tendency afoot in the behaviour of big private firms, which leads away from purely commercial considerations towards the principle of commonweal responsibility. In modern joint stock companies, which formally still adhere to the profit motive, the pursuit of profit maximization recedes into the background as a business objective. This is the central thesis of J.K. Galbraith (142). In the anonymous joint stock company, the management is chiefly interested in gross business takings as its yardstick, because it must earn normal profits to be able to pay normal dividends to shareholders and normal wages to wage-earners. It is Galbraith's view that the characteristic of modern large-scale business is that profit represents simply a means to other ends.

For that reason, it is possible to find an increasing convergence between private and commonweal large-scale enterprises, not only in the form of business activities, in their calculations of rates of return and in other factors, but even in the combinations of aims pursued by both groups.

The theory of convergence is also supported by Theo Thiemeyer, although for different reasons (143). The boundary between commonweal and private enterprise is changing, so that one can speak of a certain convergence between the types of enterprise. One of the reasons is the increasing sensitivity of large areas of public opinion to the behaviour of private business. Private enterprise will often behave in conformity with the public interest to prevent measures being taken by public authorities.

Monopolistic enterprises, moreover, do not exploit their market possibilities to the full, because they want to forestall governmental anti-trust measures. In such cases we have before us commonweal schemes carried out for reasons that have nothing to do with commonweal motivations. The same may be true of measures taken to forestall trade union actions in wage negotiations in individual enterprises and on general social issues. Private enterprise may take steps in line with the public interest to satisfy public opinion. In this case as well the increasing susceptibility of public opinion to purely private business attitudes leads, a posteriori, to the acceptance of commonweal methods. Last but not least, the management of such firms frequently behaves in the public interest to attract positive comments to satisfy their requirements for prestige.

Conversely, it might also be possible – according to Thiemeyer – for commonweal enterprises to adopt attitudes normally to be found in private business firms. This results partially from the market system. Commonweal activities on certain markets are only possible provided the firm secures a certain share in the market. Very often such a market share can only be won if the firm's capital basis is sufficiently large. For this reason there may even arise a certain compulsion on commonweal enterprises, which had renounced the profit motive because of their institutional mission to make profits. In extreme cases, this might even lead to a complete revocation of the original commonweal mission.

Whatever the reasons may be, the combinations of aims pursued by both groups, commonweal enterprise and private business, are bound to resemble each other more closely, as the enterprises increase in size. Differences between them in the end will be reduced to the simple fact that profits made by commonweal enterprise will accrue to the community in general, because these enterprises follow objectives in the general interest, whereas in private enterprise, a decreasing proportion of total profits will be acquired by private owners, because the shareholders only receive a decreasing percentage of the profits earned, while an ever increasing part will be retained by the enterprise.

Here it will be used by the management for purposes that are more in the general interest, although the fact that it is so used is often purely accidental and by no means an established intention.

We must not forget that aims pursued by commonweal and private large-scale enterprise will be modified in the long run. In times of depression private enterprise will be more willing to follow commonweal aims than in good times. On the other hand, public and commonweal enterprises will show an increasing tendency in times of growing affluence, to plough back their profits to build up reserves.

A CHANGE IN ATTITUDE AS A CONSEQUENCE OF NEW SOCIOLOGICAL CONDITIONS

Convergent behaviour in large-scale business may chiefly be attributed to sociological and social-psychological changes in society. One must start from the hypothesis that the sole application of one of the two principles, the pursuit of profit as well as the commonweal principle, is mistaken. In reality no society can ever function by adhering to one of these principles alone. Both principles should always be applied in combination. Many difficulties actually experienced by socialist states of the East can be traced back to undue neglect of aspirations to some form of personal advantage. Modern industrial societies in the West in turn can only continue to pursue the rules of private enterprise, because, at the same time, large areas in economic and social life are organized on a commonweal basis.

This dualism presupposes a society, which is sociologically differentiated with regard to these two types of behaviour. If private enterprise is to function satisfactorily, sufficient forces must be reserved to operate the commonweal system as well. In the past – according to Schumpter – representatives of pre-capitalist groups filled this gap. These were people who still maintained the necessary attitude, which they had inherited from pre-capitalist times, towards public affairs (144). Capitalism in the 19th century was a symbiosis of capitalist and feudal forces.

The bourgeoisie concentrated so much on "ledger and office affairs" that they were not able to look after the public interest themselves. This had to be done on their behalf by other elements. Capitalism, however, assimilated these protective groups to itself, and this led to the result that these groups were sooner or later unable to carry out their protective functions. Finally, there is nobody to exercise these functions of curbing the acquisitive drive. The capitalist system, therefore, becomes unbearable, and has to be abolished. "In breaking down the pre-capitalist framework of society, capitalism thus broke not only barriers that impeded its progress but also flying buttresses that prevented its collapse" (145).

Because of the destruction of the precapitalist layers, which had protected capitalism, Schumpeter predicted that the capitalist system would break down and be transformed into socialism.

In the meantime, these old layers have been replaced by new non-capitalist groups, which enter into a symbiosis with capitalism. They consist of top employees, of managers, as has been expounded by Burnham (146), of the "technostructure" as Galbraith calls them (147), as well as the growing class of intellectuals produced by a wider system of education (148). These elements fulfil, for the time being, the services which are not supplied by private enterprises pursuing their private interests.

The precapitalist classes – in Europe, patricians, aristocrats and civil servants – had derived from state socialist ideas commonweal concepts for the benefit of "the State and the Nation". They primarily created public monopolies pursuing commonweal aims. There was a variety of concepts, namely the "étatiste" paternalism in France, state enterprises in Austria and Italy and public enterprise based on municipalities in Great Britain: they were all related to the value systems of the patricians, of the nobility, and of civil servants of a precapitalist origin. In Germany, the tendency of the German Empire and the Weimar Republic towards a social state concept was based upon these attitudes; they were then misused by the Nazi system.

In accordance with their basic idea of a corporate state these groups pursued their aims through government regulation and the creation of state monopolies like the railways, the postal service and the central bank.

Managers and intellectuals of the late capitalist era, however, behave in a different way. Their ideas are no longer based on the national state and on legal conceptions; they tend towards supra-national cooperation and towards the social and natural sciences. These groups think not so much in terms of institutions as of functions. The public monopoly type of enterprise with commonweal obligations, corresponds less to their world of ideas than does the "free" commonweal enterprise. It also accords with the mentality and the interests of these modern managerial groups to subject commercial enterprises more and more to commonweal responsibilities, thus approximating them to commonweal enterprises.

Late capitalist groups of this kind will not adapt their mental outlook to traditional business ways, as pre-capitalist groups did. They will not be taken over by it. On the contrary they will transmit their value code to the old order, instead of allowing it to shape them, and they will increasingly determine the intellectual atmosphere of society.

Chapter 16

COMPETITIVE FUNCTIONS OF COMMONWEAL ENTERPRISE

Commonweal enterprises of the German workers' movement do business within the framework of a competitive market system, such as exists in most countries of the Western world. The struggle for survival dominates nature as a whole. The struggle between economic forces, i.e. competition, is but a particular case of the social struggle in general. Competition, in actual act, is imposed by nature for biological reasons; we may, therefore, conclude that it is beyond the power of mankind to decide whether there ought to be competition, or whether it ought to disappear (149). It is quite possible to equalize needs and at the same time to suppress the tendency of humans to surpass one another. One must, moreover, be able to satisfy fully all needs in kind and quantity. Since none of these three conditions is ever satisfied, and as it is not probable that they will ever be satisfied, competition remains one of the bases of our existence (150).

No society will ever exist without competition (151). It is, therefore, society's task to utilize the numerous differences existing between people by combining them within a system based upon its proper principles. Perfect competition constitutes at the same time both a measuring rod and an aim. In addition it acts as a selection process and exercises an educational influence. Competition stimulates creative activities, which contribute in turn towards further development. At the same time, through imitation, competition "socializes" peak achievements to the benefit of all. If competition was considered an aberration for many centuries, this was due to numerous distortions, which occurred in the course of history, especially to monopolistic practices of a social and economic kind. These latter practices brought about by the prevalence of petty interests of small groups or even individuals led time and again to a breakdown of competition.

Today, we may consider that the debate about the task competition has to fulfil in society is closed. Competition reduces costs, increases productivity, adapts production to effective demand and is ready to fill any deficiency in supply. Competition introduces and tests new goods, new production methods and new lines (152). Without a high degree of competition between enterprises there will be little freedom of choice, and it will also be very difficult to protect the right to a free choice of employment. Both these important basic rights in a free society are themselves part and parcel of competition.

An important task of commonweal enterprises consists in regulating competition. We consider that commonweal enterprises have to protect competition against distortion, direct it in such a way that it serves the common good, and produce the best possible supply of goods and services for the population. In the following text we demonstrate this briefly in the case of well-known forms of market failure. Subsequently the functions of a commonweal enterprise in a dynamic competitive process is described.

COMMONWEAL ENTERPRISES UNDER MONOPOLISTIC MARKET CONDITIONS

Whenever markets are dominated for technical reasons by a monopoly it will in most cases be in the hands of the community. This is mostly the case with technically conditioned "grid" monopolies (153): gas, water, electricity and heating supply, communications and all rail transportation systems. This is the domain of public control, which requires the monopoly to behave as if competition prevailed. The prices of goods and services offered are in principle based on costs; very often, public utilities are obliged to renounce price increases, which are economically necessary, because political considerations intervene.

In such cases, the principle of meeting needs predominates, but this does not exclude the possibility that the necessary share of internal funds for investment will be obtained through appropriate pricing. On the other hand it may be possible to renounce any interest payable on owner's equity, because such a renunciation, or general non-profitmaking attitude, will not result in ruinous competition with private competitors. The latter result would be inevitable in fully competitive or oligopolistic markets.

Taxation is also superfluous in such cases. A mixed enterprise, in the sense of a combined public/private partnership, is not very suitable either in such markets, as such firms will have to respect the private capitalists' point of view, and this will conflict with their public utility function (154). The principle of price discrimination, which is part of monopolistic pricing, can be applied in such cases to attain economic and social goals, instead of being used for private profit maximization.

Public "grid" monopolies are undeniably monopolistic with regard to their suppliers. Their commonweal character, however, prevents the exploitation of monopoly power. They are obliged to organize a competitive system in their purchasing procedure. This deters their suppliers from any specialization on the products demanded by one of these firms, and thus maintains the supplier's independence. The type of purchasing policy also hinders the creation of countervailing monopolies, which would then invade other markets.

COMMONWEAL ENTERPRISES IN CONDITIONS OF ATOMISTIC COMPETITION

Atomistic competition is the counterpart of monopoly, for in society perfect competition is not in fact the counterpart of monopolistic or oligopolistic competition. We find on the contrary a system of atomistic competition in many markets, where numerous small entrepreneurs appear as suppliers, quoting traditional trade margins and maintaining a traditional rent or price level, while hardly taking account of actual costs.

In atomistic competition two departures from actual costs are possible: producers or traders may offer their goods and services either considerably above or considerably below total cost. In the first case atomistic competition assumes a parasitic character and in the second, a cut-throat one.

Cooperative societies are supposed to counteract such distortions of the competitive process: cooperatives of independent traders and artisans, and purchase, sales and credit cooperatives are to apply methods that conform to the rules of the market economy to eliminate cut-throat competition, while cooperatives of workers, tenants and consumers, i.e. housing and consumers' cooperatives, attempt to correct parasitic competition by applying methods conforming to market principles.

In both cases government intervention is not of much avail. A government policy directed towards the middle-classes cannot be applied in the case of cut-throat competition, as can be done in social policy, agricultural policy, and transport policy etc., because measures designed by the state to further middle-class interests tend to break down. If a system of protection is created for this type of undertaking, there appear immediately numerous new firms attracted by the assurance of higher profits. This intensifies the competition and undermines the protective measures. Government middle-class policy, if carried out seriously, must always resemble a race between a hare and a tortoise. It will only succeed if accompanied by a licencing system limiting access to the various trades, no matter whether these limitations exist formally, or whether the limitation exists from the nature of things. Any such formal licence system, however, runs counter to the principles of a market system, and contradicts the principle of the free exercise of trade and industry.

In this sphere, fiscal aid to help with capital formation by the owner is within limits, the only form of support that corresponds to the principles of the system. Otherwise, these enterprises have to resort to mutual aid systems, through commonweal enterprises and in particular through cooperatives. The competitive tasks of cooperative societies consist in encouraging weak business units to maintain their position and efficiency in the competition that is essential to a market economy.

"The combination of certain individual business functions in collective cooperative enterprises leads to an assured and stronger market position for member units, so that small and medium-size member units in particular will have a chance to hold their ground, maintain their stability and develop under competitive conditions. Furthermore, member units will be offered the opportunity by combining under cooperative principles, to exploit to an increasing degree, all the economic advantages to be derived from business specialization and rationalization, even for the functions which have not been organized in this way. In such a way advantages that normally accrue only to large enterprises will be accessible to smaller firms, with whom the large compete. In this manner, cooperative societies exercise a (commonweal – W.H) equalizing function in the capitalist market economy" (155).

Cooperative societies strengthen the market position of many small units. By combining the individual functions of member units, cooperative societies can exercise some influence on prices on behalf of their members and counteract the ruinous operation of competition. Furthermore, they offer advantages arising from the decreasing costs in large-scale production, which is of increasing importance given the increasing capital intensity of production. Whenever members of a cooperative encounter original market power, the cooperative organizations help them to create countervailing power. In doing so they increase the intensity of competition, to the benefit of all (156).

Many cooperatives, buying, selling, credit and others, are able to combine business activities that are particularly suited to separate business units, because of sharply decreasing costs. Even if this leads to the formation of large societies, it does not constitute a contradiction to cooperative philosophy. At any rate complete independence does not exist in economic life. An independent artisan, from whom a cooperative takes over much of the trouble and a good deal of work, is very often much more independent in the remainder of his business activities than another independent worker, who despite great efforts does not escape from the red. Unprofitability creates the worst form of dependence.

In the case of "parasitic competition" as with cut-throat competition, very little can be done by government methods. As soon as the rent and price level settles down under atomistic competition at a level considerably above average costs in spite of a vast number of suppliers, government price or rent fixing can only constitute a short-term solution. Government price fixing systems entail awkward consequences, in that goods disappear under the counter, and "grey" and "black" markets arise. Soon such systems have to be complemented by government rationing schemes for houses and goods. At the end of a chain of coercive measures we then find a rationing system with vouchers, closely resembling the systems used during both world wars and in the years following the Second World War.

Even in the case of parasitic competition, the most effective method consists in mutual aid by means of commonweal enterprises, formed by those concerned and conforming to the rules of the market economy. In this case tenants and consumers will form housing societies and consumers' cooperatives, or public utility housing companies. The activities of such societies have already been described in detail in the chapters dealing with the groups "co-op" and "Neue Heimat".

COMMONWEAL ENTERPRISES UNDER OLIGOPOLISTIC CONDITIONS

All these categories of enterprises, consumers' cooperatives and trade union enterprises such as "Volksfürsorge", "Neue Heimat' and the "Bank für Gemeinwirtschaft", work today increasingly in conditions of oligopoly.

In such markets, a few big enterprises establish an unstable equilibrium, from which none is interested in moving to a system of real price competition. Because oligopolists are in most cases in quite a strong financial position, a struggle for power would soon turn into ruinous competition for all of them. They, therefore, prefer a policy of trial and error, and hold back on supply, so that prices will remain high enough to permit formation of oligopoly profit for the majority of oligopolists. (There are markets where oligopolists still make good profits, in spite of the fact that capacity is only utilized to the extent of sixty per cent). Such an oligopoly profit is indeed unstable, but it may persist over a long period and provide receipts for the owner that are by no means justified in terms of services offered, and would never accrue to him under conditions of keener competition. These receipts in turn are earned at the expense of consumers. Besides, oligopolists shun price competition and turn to product differentiation, advertising and the like, which distort competition. As a consequence the distributive function of competition is undermined in the same way as its function of allocating resources. Prices will be inflated, because of oligopolistic tendencies, and will no longer serve as a yardstick of scarcity. The inevitable consequence of all this must be misdirection of capital and labour.

The government can only remedy this in a very limited way. First of all, the authorities very often do not understand the necessity of taking appropriate steps, or they do not want to understand. Exploitation by oligopolies and misdirection of labour and capital caused by them do not appear so distinctly as they would under conditions of atomistic competition.

For instance, when there was an opportunity, in 1958, to change the "Volkswagenwerk" into a commonweal enterprise – as had been envisaged at the time of its foundation (157) – this proposal was dropped in the German Diet, without any discussion (158). This probably happened, because such a proposal was still quite alien to the ideas professed by all groups involved in economic policy at that time. A good many people who were responsible for economic policy in the fifties or sixties, still thought that business activities were a purely private affair (159). If oligopolistic distortion of competition is recognized today by men responsible for economic policy, measures designed to counteract it are generally of a purely legislative character consisting in anti-cartel laws and the prohibition of cartels. Even if such laws are very important and their relevance must not be underrated, judicial and important administrative shortcomings within the framework of such systems do indeed diminish their effectiveness very considerably.

On the other hand, commonweal enterprises are quite appropriate means of fostering competition even within oligopolitic markets. In these markets in particular they have to fulfil important tasks. They can act as automatic stabilizers here, and maintain competition through swift actions conforming to the principles of the market economy.

B. Molitor once sketched for public enterprise a simple model of an automatic stabilizer in this sense. He wrote: "Public enterprise should primarily fulfil the task of exercising persistent pressure on prices, assuming in this way a function normally exercised by the automatic working of the market forces in perfect competition. A public enterprise will normally try to reduce its costs in the same way as its competitors do, by exploiting technical progress. It will also try to increase its sales volume, being inspired by efficiency considerations, and in doing so it will apply the same entrepreneurial methods (including a minimum of self-financing) as other enterprises do. There will, however, be one decisive exception – i.e. its price strategy will not be aimed at profit maximisation, but at price decreases or at least at a regulative influence on prices" (160). The tasks thus assigned to public enterprise as instruments of public policy on oligopolistic markets, and especially as instruments of competition policy, may well be ascribed to all commonweal enterprises including the "free" sector.

COMMONWEAL ENTERPRISES IN DYNAMIC COMPETITION

If we investigate the rôle commonweal enterprises can play in competition, it will not be enough to deal only with price competition. In examining only one aspect of competition from a single viewpoint, we deprive ourselves of the possibility of presenting a great number of important rôles open to commonweal enterprise in competitive processes. We must, therefore, now leave the domain of the classic forms of competition and choose conceptions of competition for our investigation that do not only take pricing into consideration. This new backdrop includes the competition of substitutes of new products, of new techniques, of new sources of supply, and of new types of organization, for instance, the transition towards big enterprise; it will therefore include that kind of competition "which commands a decisive cost or quality advantage and which strikes not at the margins of the profits and the outputs of the existing firms, but at their foundations and their very lives" (161).

Economic life is nowadays dominated by dynamic competitive processes, and the classic forms of competition will only occur in marginal cases; this is exemplified in two diametrically opposed forms. "Competitors can either imitate what others have introduced and thereby undermine the advantage which the innovators have won. Or they can surpass the others by the excellence of their achievements and clear the field of rivals . . . The first type of competition can be classed as 'the competition of the imitator' and the second "the competition of the innovator' " (162). The competition of the innovator will bring about further differentiation, because he is more capable or uses existing facilities in a better way. This form of competition aims at monopoly. On the other hand, we encounter "the competition of the imitator", which levels existing differences, and removes the monopoly positions held by innovators. The process of competition arises from the reaction between these two poles and if the innovators and imitators complement each other's activities, both processes may go on forever. In this way improvements and innovations will be stimulated and soon become generalized through the competition of imitators. They see to it that possible innovations are made and put into use for the benefit of the general public by means of price reductions, quality improvements, cost reductions etc. (163).

COMMONWEAL ENTERPRISES AS INNOVATORS

Public enterprises have always been innovators, in some cases pursuing commonweal aims as we understand them today. We need only recall the economic activities of mercantilist states. In many cases the governments of such states initiated industrialization. Similar developments are taking place today in almost all developing countries. During the 19th century the predominance of liberal ideas led to a limitation of economic activities to transportation, gas, electricity and water supply. In these branches, public enterprise nevertheless contributed to the greatest achievements of the time, notably railway construction.

A large number of public enterprises came into being during the First World War through the initiative of the state. Inventions and innovations made by these enterprises subsequently stimulated technical development. This process was repeated in the thirties, when on top of the rearmament policy was added the desire for autarky. The result was in many respects the same as during the First World War. In the fifties and sixties, atomic energy was the most important area of development. The capital requirement is so great, that from the outset this sector has been in public control and is a field of commonweal activity in our sense, although during this decade conventional economic wisdom has been hostile to state activities.

Today, autarkical tendencies are no longer generally approved of in developed industrial countries. Instead of the national state striving for autarky, the democratic welfare state comes to the forefront. Ideas of national power have receded and government control is, instead, primarily appreciated from the point of view of the general welfare and the security, which it offers to its citizens. For this reason, attainment of a high and steady rate of growth becomes the most important goal pursued by the state. This obliges the state to take measures to secure and guarantee a high growth rate. Commonweal enterprises are ideally suited to be the instruments essential for a realization of this important goal of state activity. They can help by finding new ways of production, by testing inventions and improvements made elsewhere, and by applying them as quickly as possible to their own industry. In our times and at the stage of industrialization reached in Western Europe, knowledge and know-how have become in many cases more important than capital and hard work.

Commonweal enterprises are particularly suited, from an economic point of view, to act as innovators in the competitive process, because they are not likely to make capital out of any advantage which accrues to them from new technical processes. They are not, as it happens allowed to establish permanent monopoly positions, for they have to follow the rules laid down in their statutes, and, therefore, eliminate any possible monopoly profit by augmenting their supply.

They may also have comprehensive obligations of publicity imposed upon them, to make the task of the imitator easier.

Commonweal enterprises, since their very foundation, have contributed to the competition of the imitator. Some cases are well-known, as for example, when they introduced modern forms of enterprise and progressive methods of production into frontier and development areas. Cooperatives, in particular, frequently exercised such functions in addition to acts of innovatory character. Whenever individual firms lacked knowledge and capital, cooperatives would open up purchase, sales and credit possibilities for large groups of the working-class and of the middle-class in towns and in the countryside possibilities, which the private dealer would offer only under exceptional circumstances. Perfabricated construction was introduced into house building through public utility housing companies. This is a further modern example of productive imitation. The management of commonweal enterprises is institutionally linked to consumers' interests, and this awakes the need to introduce new methods from elsewhere sooner than is the case with a private profit-seeking firm, for as a rule it does not attempt to maximize profits but merely to earn a normal level of profits, a situation which is particularly true of the traditional middle-class entrepreneur.

THE CONDITION: COMPETITIVE SIZE

If the commonweal enterprise is effectively to fulfil its rôle in free competition, it must dispose of a sufficient share of the market and be able to expand in the same way as other firms in the same branch of activity. The larger part of its stock ought to be in the hands of public authorities of "free" social associations. Jointly owned enterprises are often impeded by all sorts of considerations in the fulfilment of their tasks.

If commonweal enterprise is to foster competition, it ought not to operate under conditions which are more or less favourable than those which private enterprise faces.

After all, within the framework of their objectives, commonweal enterprises require as much independence as private enterprises, and they must bear their losses themselves. They have no reason to claim subsidies as a natural right. Whenever the enterprises need new financial resources, they must get them from the capital market as any other enterprise must and under the same conditions. As a general rule, they have little prospect of obtaining new equity capital on the free market. Their only possibility consists in getting capital from individuals or free associations, whose interests in society are the same as theirs. This means that commonweal enterprises are at a disadvantage, compared with their competitors. They are not, however, subject to the requirement that high profits must be made for their owners. Their only obligation consists in paying a normal return on the capital of their founders, a remuneration corresponding more or less to the current rate of interest in the country concerned.

Chapter 17

THE LIMITS AND TASKS OF COMMONWEAL ENTERPRISES IN THE SOCIAL GROWTH PROCESS

Today, the market systems in the Euro-American industrialization model are undergoing new developments. They open new tasks and new possibilities to commonweal enterprise, but at the same time they set new limits.

LIMITS TO COMMONWEAL ENTERPRISES

It is not only opponents who constitute a danger to progressive ideas. Even their protagonists run the risk of jeopardizing them by harbouring excessive expectations. Such illusions make it easier for adversaries to oppose them, for they mislead their protagonists into making excessive claims for young establishments, and finally provoke bitter disappointment among their adherents, when the establishments fail to live up to these exaggerated expectations. We may, therefore, still mention some tasks, the fulfilment of which is not primarily the responsibility of commonweal enterprise.

Let us first examine the simplest case. It is by no means possible to charge public and commonweal enterprise both with regulative tasks, and also with other responsibilities, and expect them to earn revenue for the state budget or the budget of particular social associations which these enterprises own. If one requires them to make profits, there will be a conflict with their inherent commonweal objectives.

Secondly, one misunderstands the function of commonweal enterprises if one requires them to prevent the operation of the selective function of competition, by laying upon them the task of supporting unviable sectors of industry. "Capitalism, then, is by nature a form or method of economic change . . . The fundamental impulse that sets and keeps the capitalist engine in motion comes from the new consumers' goods, the new methods of production or transportation, the new markets, the new forms of industrial organization that capitalist enterprise creates."

It is a process of discontinuous industrial change "that incessantly revolutionizes the economic structure from within, incessantly destroying the old one, incessantly creating a new one. The process of creative destruction is the essential fact about capitalism" (164).

Commonweal enterprises must never try to oppose such forces by regarding themselves as instruments of a misunderstood conservative or even restorative economic policy. On the contrary, such enterprises will have to fulfil an essential task of social policy, namely the absorption of labour released during the process of "creative destruction".

Furthermore, to quote a third misunderstanding, commonweal enterprises cannot be innovators in social spheres, if this leads to a considerable increase in costs. Higher wage costs will impede their commonweal tasks, especially their competitive functions. These are directed at price reductions or price stabilization, and through such means, at an increase in the purchasing power of mainly lower income groups. Their social functions embrace the whole economy, being oriented towards the consumers' interests. They are not concerned with particular interests, no matter whether it is a question of staff interests or of municipal interests, i.e. of the municipality, in which the enterprise has its headquarters (165). If these commonweal enterprises succeed in stimulating competition in their economic sector, their activities have the direct effect of maintaining a scarcity of labour, which enables the trade unions to improve the working conditions of labour generally. Commonweal enterprises ought to contribute towards the destruction of privileges even in the labour market, and they should not help to create new privileged positions. This does not exclude the possibility of setting an example in their own business organizations, in their attitude towards worker-participation and in the relationship between management and staff: all this is part of their competitive function.

In this context, we must mention yet another subsidiary task, which is very often ascribed to commonweal enterprises: namely their contribution towards stabilization policy, in which they are expected to carry out an anti-cyclical price and investment policy. Such a policy also is not compatible with their commonweal objectives in many cases. Whenever people demand that commonweal enterprises conduct an anti-cyclical pricing policy, they too easily forget that very often such a policy leads to the technical backwardness of such enterprises, whenever the state has exercised pressure on public monopolies to get them to behave in this way. For commonweal enterprises that are exposed to competition, there are even fewer possibilities for applying such a policy. Such enterprises can only try to set a good example by giving support to general measures of business cycle policy. Since they are anyway under an obligation to take account of the common good, the autonomy of their management need not be jeopardized by these additional tasks. On the contrary, their intimate knowledge of the peculiarities of the sectors in which they operate, offers a good counterweight to the attitude of ministries responsible for economic policy, for these ministries are liable to stick too stubbornly to ideas based on purely macro-economic considerations.

COMMONWEAL ENTERPRISES AND GOVERNMENT INTERVENTION

Whenever global indicative planning is introduced to a basically competitive system, or whenever such a system supplements a competitive system, the functions of commonweal enterprises are not essentially modified. They will, however, become much more important. For any system of national accounting and especially in any planning for its future, realistic prices and price relationships are an essential condition. This problem occurs in any private concern, when it fixes accounting prices to assess its position and to trace possible sources of loss. Commonweal enterprises can assist government agencies in their work by furnishing all necessary information. The efficiency of government intervention depends very largely upon a regular stream of first class information, which must be easily available to the ministries concerned. Government intervention in an essentially private economy presupposes the existence, in each sector, of "pilot" enterprises suitable for serving as test cases. The responsibility of informing other agencies is not a task these enterprises have to fulfil only with regard to the government. They should also keep the general public informed and they should extend their information services to include all problems that could be of public interest.

Some state-owned commonweal enterprises, which are not primarily concerned with competition policy – generally public transport, gas, water and electricity supply – may be able to carry out a supracyclical investment policy, within the framework of a growth policy at which all planning measures are directed. Such a long-term investment policy based on a planned expansion may be undertaken within a national plan, and in so far as this is possible, may have a lasting effect on the supply industries of that firm (166). On the other hand, such commonweal enterprises will have to receive subsidies from the government out of government deficit spending in recession years (167). In this way, they may serve as an instrument of a planning system that aims at fostering long-term growth.

It must be admitted that such a policy would not be reasonable if it were to be applied to "free" commonweal enterprise operating in a competitive environment. In doing so one would misunderstand their primary rôle of competing with private firms, and such a policy would contradict the principle of fair competition. In spite of that, these enterprises might still be able to render inestimable services to public authorities by assisting them in the same way as within the framework of business cycles policies, so long as this did not contradict their competitive tasks. At the same time, the rôle of innovator in the competitive process remains the most important task for commonweal enterprises, even in an economic system that is increasingly subject to governmental direction, no matter whether the Zeitgeist of the particular period favours competition or governmental intervention.

COMMONWEAL ENTERPRISES AND NON-GOVERNMENTAL SPHERES OF LIFE

The commonweal enterprises under consideration arose as mutual-aid institutions founded by members of oppressed social groups. A new type of enterprise originated from the initiative of independent social groups, with the function of a stabilizer in the process of competition and of a pioneer for new, socially desirable, objectives. It represents an independent instrument of an economic policy that favours consumers and the social aspects of life in general.

This new type of enterprise will be all the more necessary, as economic and social developments get more and more complex. It is no longer possible to maintain such developments on a steady path, desirable as this is from the point of view of society, merely by applying the methods of competition, legislation and fiscal policy. The more market conditions are changed, and oligopolies fostered by the growth of firms and the increasing capital intensity of production, the more the latent forces of stagnation will gain in strength, the more necessary will autonomous forces be within a free competitive system to counteract any sort of fossilization. Again, developed industrial countries will have to solve tasks that cannot be solved by private enterprise, and in many cases "free" commonweal enterprises will be better able than government agencies to deal with such problems.

Through the activities of commonweal enterprises, a sphere of life is developing that will remain free from government intervention. Their operation in the public interest makes state intervention unnecessary. It is for this reason that those circles that reject government intervention in economic life should avail themselves of this type of enterprise, which has been developed by municipalities, cooperatives and trade unions. Whoever wants freedom from government intervention should see to it that other social forces establish commonweal enterprises.

Because of their business ideal of looking after the consumers' interests, enterprises run by such free social forces not only secure economic freedom for consumers, but also – paradoxical though it seems – for private entrepreneurs, by helping them to preserve their freedom of action, by rendering government intervention superfluous. This function of creating and maintaining freedom is particularly applicable to commonweal enterprises of the consumers' cooperative movement and of the workers' movement in general, since both represent majorities and not minorities, as do, for example, industrial associations. On the other hand, they can only fulfil their obligation to act on behalf of the majority by defending the common good.

NEW TASKS IN THE GROWTH PROCESS

Orientated as they are towards the common good, commonweal enterprises are destined within the sphere that is free from government interference to solve new tasks in new social circumstances. Theirs is especially the task of offering an alternative to private business in the face of new social forces and new conditions, and to represent and test forms of behaviour that might be those of the future.

The central importance of the commonweal economy in relation to the future, lies in the fact that development tends more and more towards the acceptance of public and commonweal obligations by private business as well. The "law of increasing government activity", which was conceived by Adolph Wagner, remains as true as it was in his day, a hundred years ago. The tendency underlying this law continues to prevail today.

The assumption that the importance of the commonweal economy is bound to increase in future is founded on three different trends. First of all, there is the phenomenon of increasing concentration, which holds true of single firms, enterprises, groups and of trusts. These developments arise not only from technical considerations, but since the arrival of the computer they are also relevant from an administrative point of view.

The tendency towards concentration has been largely conditioned by increasing risks, accelerating technical progress and, last but not least, by bigger markets. Today, more and more firms are obliged to produce for international markets, which cannot be easily disregarded, but they contain a great number of political, and sometimes even currency, risks.

Again, the modern big business is of such national importance that governments cannot allow it to go bankrupt and are obliged to help it whenever it gets into difficulties. The modern state frequently even helps big business in its development stage in many ways. When the lives of such firms are over, the government helps them in the difficult operation of reducing scale and closing down. The state is obliged to act in this manner to avoid inestimable damage at the political and economic level. In the reality of modern society private big business has long been a national institution and more and more firms develop into large enterprises and, therefore, tend to become national institutions.

The second reason underlying the assertion that commonweal economy has a bright future, lies in the transition from the naive laisser-faire market economy to an enlightened growth-conscious planned economic policy – i.e. planning in an indicative manner. Such an economic policy, comprising a package of monetary, administrative and fiscal measures, is intended to bring about optimum growth while safeguarding price stability and external equilibrium within the framework of the so-called "magic square". This means that entrepreneurial risks will be greatly diminished, for it will always be quite evident which sectors are open to development, and these will be systematically fostered. Entrepreneurial risks will, furthermore, be considerably diminished through such a growth-conscious economic policy, because other sectors, where no further growth is or should be possible, will also become quite evident. Now, economic policy will not only see to it that cutbacks in these sectors take place in a civilized manner, but it will even speed up trends towards contraction to release manpower needed for growth industries, for this is implied in a policy of stimulating growth.

All this signifies that the autonomy of entrepreneurs will be effectively and essentially limited, and that their risks will also be diminished. Both these trends tend to reduce the applicability and the importance of the principles of private and competitive business. It is not out of the question that both trends, towards concentration and towards growth-conscious indicative planning, will deprive big business of its legitimacy. It is quite conceivable that private ownership of the means of production in large enterprises and private use of profit will become increasingly unsatisfactory from a social standpoint. Large scale enterprise will, therefore, be more and more subject to commonweal objectives.

Over and above these two reasons explaining a tendency towards the progressive transition of privately managed large firms to commonweal objectives, there is a third reason: the increasing democratization of Western society in all aspects of life. This tendency will not permit profits, which often bear no relationship to the services rendered, to continue to be appropriated by a small group of people. The bitterness of the debate on the wider ownership of capital bears witness to such a tendency.

Slowly but surely and almost imperceptibly, the Western economic system will transform itself into a commonweal system, and move away from private enterprise. The period of reconstruction following the Second World War was only a "shortened recapitulation of earlier capitalist conditions", for everything had to be rebuilt within a very short space of time. Taken by itself, this period was adequate and useful. We must not, however, determine our perspective of the future by what happened during these two decades. The pendulum is swinging more and more in the direction of commonweal forms of business, not least because they represent a superior economic rational reasoning. Today, it is quite possible to develop a new industrial system without creating a new bourgeoisie depending, as it does, on market contingencies and accidental heritage. The creation of such a new system had already been conceived by Karl Marx, and Joseph Schumpeter, the great German conservative economist, who also foresaw that it would come.

In his book "The New Industrial State" the American economist Galbraith has recently argued the same thesis in a very convincing way (168).

The theory of increasing state activity and of the growing importance of commonweal considerations in the productive activities of large-scale enterprise does not signify that it will not be possible to leave vast areas of economic life to private business in future. Private production will retain its full justification, wherever small and medium size enterprise represent the optimum size. We must envisage the possibility, however, that within the next generation it will no longer be the determining influence shaping the face, the dynamics and the social climate of our time. I welcome the progressive growth of commonweal forms of enterprise in future, because it relies on altruistic tendencies present in mankind.

If man were unable to direct himself towards humane objectives, and could only survive by following selfish aims, then our future, in spite of advanced technical development, would indeed offer a bleak and apocalyptic outlook.

Notes

1 See F.G. Weisser, *Form und Wesen der Einzelwirtschaften, Theorie und Politik ihrer Stile* (*Form and Essence of Individual Economic Units – Theory and Policy of their Styles*), Vol. I, 2nd edition, Göttingen 1949. Also: G. Weisser, "Die Lehre von den gemeinnützigen Unternehmen" ("The Theory of Public Utility Enterprise"), *Archiv für öffentliche und freigemeinwirtschaftliche Unternehmen*, ..., Vol. I (1954).

2 See H. Ritschl, *Gemeinwirtschaft und Kapitalistische Marktwirtschaft (Commonweal Economy and Capitalist Market Economy)*, Tübingen, 1931. Also: Ritschl, "Die Prinzipien der Gemeinwirtschaft" ("The Principles of Commonweal Economy"), in W. Weddingen (editor), *Untersuchungen zur sozialen Gestaltung der Wirtschaftsordnung* (*Research into the Social Concept of Economic Order*), Schriften des Vereins für Sozialpolitik (Publications of the Association for Social Policy), N.F. Vol. 2, Berlin, p. 1–43.

3 The following text is based upon the articles "Gemeinwirtschaft" ("Commonweal Economy") by H. Ritschl and "Sozialisierung I" ("Socialization I") by G. Rittig in the *Handwörterbuch der Sozialwissenschaften* (*Dictionary of the Social Sciences*). Further articles quoted are: "Gemeinwirtschaft" ("Commonweal Economy") by H.E. Littmann in *Handwöarterbuch der Betriebswirtschaft* (*Dictionary of Management Economics*) and "Eigenunternehmen der Gewerkschaften" ("Enterprises of the Trade Unions") by W. Astor, "Gemeinwirtschaft (Christliche Gewerkschaften"), ("Commonweal Economy – Christian Trade Unions") by J. Jahn and "Gemeinwirtschaft (Freie Gewerkschaften)" – ("Commonweal Economy – Free Trade Unions") by F. Naphtali; all of them published in the *Internationales Handwörterbuch des Gewerkschaftswesens* (*International Manual of Trade-Unionism*), Berlin, 1931.

4 F.B.W. von Hermann, *Staatswirtschaftliche Untersuchungen über Vermögen, Wirtschaft, Produktivität der Arbeiten, Kapital, Preis, Gewinn, Einkommen und Verbrauch* (*Economic Research into Property, Economy, Productivity of Work, Capital, Prices, Profits, Income and Consumption*), Munich, 1832; reprint of the first edition, Leipzig, 1924.

5 See W. Roscher, *System der Volkswirtschaft* (*System of National Economy*), Vol. I–V, Stuttgart, 1854; new edition, edited by R. Pöhlmann, 1922.

6 See A.E.F. Schäffle, *Die Nationalökonomie oder allgemeine Wirtschaftslehre* (*The National Economy or General Science of Economics*), Leipzig, 1861, 2nd Edition under the title *Das gesellschaftliche System der menschlichen Wirtschaft* (*The Social System of Human Economy*), Tübingen, 1867.

7 See Th. Thiemeyer, "Im Wechselspiel der Theorie" ("The Fluctuation of Theory") in Special edition of the journal *Volkswirt*, No. 50, (Partner und Konkurrent" – "Partnership and Competition") of 15th December 1967, pp.

5–7; see also Thiemeyer, "Gemeinnützigkeit als Ordnungsprinzip" ("Public Utility as a Principle of Order"), Ph. D. thesis, Cologne, 1960, mimeographed manuscript, p. 28 et seq.

8 See C. Landauer, "Sozialismus III" ("Socialism III") in *Handwörterbuch der Sozialwissenschaften* (*Dictionary of Social Sciences*), Vol. 9, pp. 499–501.

9 See L. von Mises, *Die Gemeinwirtschaft, Untersuchung über den Sozialismus*, (*Commonweal Economy, an Analysis of Socialism*), Jena, 2nd edition 1932, also Mises, "Wirtschaftsrechnung im sozialistischen Gemeinwesen" ("Economic Calculus in a Socialist Community"), in *Archiv für Sozialwissenschaft und Sozialpolitik* (*Archives for Social Science and Social Policy*), Vol. 47 (1920).

10 See L.J. Zimmermann, *Geschichte der theoretischen Volkswirtschaftslehre* (*History of Theoretical Economics*), Cologne, 1954, p. 106; and C. Landauer, Sozialismus II (*Socialism III*), op. cit., p. 495.

11 Cf. A. Wagner, *Lehr – und Handbuch der politischen Ökonomie*, I. Hauptabt.: "Grundlegung der politischen Ökonomie" (*Manual and Treatise on Political Economy*, I. section: "Foundations of Political Economy"), 1st part, Leipzig 1892 and 1893, reprint 1925, 2nd part, 1894.

12 Cf. M. Cassel, *Die Gemeinwirtschaft, ihre Stellung und Notwendigkeit in der Tauschwirtschaft* (*Commonweal Economy – Its Position and Necessity in an Exchange System*), Leipzig, 1925.

13 Cf. H. Ritschl, *Die Prinzipien der Gemeinwirtschaft* (*Principles of Commonweal Economy*), op. cit.

14 Cf. A. Ammon, "Zur Grundlegung einer Theorie der öffentlichen Gemeinwirtschaft", in *Festgabe für Dr. H. Schorer*, ("Foundation of a Theory of the Public Commonweal Economy" in *Publication in Honour of Dr. H. Schorer*), Bern, 1947.

15 Cf. G. Weisser, "Einzelwirtschaftspolitik. Die gemeinwirtschaftlichen Unternehmen als Subjekte und Objekte der Politik", ("Economic Policy for Individual Economic Units. Commonweal Enterprise as Subjects and Objects of Policy"), *Ökonomische und sozialpolitische Themen zur Gemeinwirtschaft"* (*Economic and Social Themes concerning Commonweal Economy*), Festschrift für E. Milhaud, (Publication in Honour of E. Milhaud), Liège, 1960, p. 75.

16 Cf. W. Sombart, *Sozialismus und soziale Bewegung im 19. Jahrhundert*, (*Socialism and Social Movement in the 19th century*), Jena, 1896, quoted in its new edition, Vienna, 1966, p. 31.

17 Apostles 2: 44, 45; 4: 32–35 in the New Testament.

18 Cf. E. Salin, *Politische Ökonomie* (*Political Economy*) Tübingen/Zürich, 1967, p. 94 et seq.

19 Cf. L.J. Zimmerman, op. cit., p. 87 et seq.

20 Cf. W. Hofmann, *Ideengeschichte der sozialen Bewegung des 19. und 20. Jahrhunderts* (*History of Ideas of the Social Movement of the 19th and 20th Centuries*), 2nd revised and enlarged edition, with the collaboration of W. Abendroth, Berlin, 1968, pp. 19 and 20.

21 E. Bloch, *Das Prinzip Hoffnung* (*The Principle of Hope*), Frankfurt, 1959.

22 H. Faust, *Genossenschaftliches Lesebuch, Zeugnisse aus hundert Jahren, (Cooperative Manual, Testimonials from the Last One Hundred Years)*, Frankfurt, 1957, quoted from a preface written by Faust, p. 11.

23 *Statuten und Geschäftsordnung des Internationalen Genossenschaftsbundes* (*Statutes and Standing Orders of the International Cooperative Alliance*), edited by its Central Office, 11, Upper Grovenor Street, London, W.1, 1966, p. 1. See also: W. W. Engelhardt, "Wandlungen und Reformen der deutschen Konsumgenossenschaften", ("Changes and Reforms in German Consumers' Cooperative Societies"), in *Schmollers Jahrbuch*, 88th year, (1968), p. 301.

24 Cf. S. and B. Webb, "Die genossenschaftliche Gemeinwirtschaft" ("The

Cooperative Commonwealth"), translated from *The Consumers' Cooperative Movement*, Halberstadt, 1924.

25 Cf. E. Pfeiffer, *Uber Genossenschaftswesen; was ist der Arbeiterstand und was kann er werden?* (*On the Cooperative System – What is the Working Class, and What can it Become?*), Leipzig, 1863.

26 Cf. Ch. Gide, "Les Sociétés Coopératives de Consommation" ("The Consumers' Cooperative Societies"), Paris, 1924. German: "Der Kooperatismus", in *Soziale Organisation der Gegenwart* (*Social Organization of the Present*), Halberstadt, 1929.

27 Cf. R. Wilbrandt, "Die Bedeutung der Konsumgenossenschaften" ("The Meaning of Consumers' Cooperative Societies"), Göttingen, 1915, in *Kapitalismus und Konsumenten* (*Capitalism and Consumers*), Konsumvereinspolitik GdS., IX. 2., Tübingen, 1927, the same article appeared in *Konsumgenossenschaften* (*Consumers' Cooperative Societies*), Stuttgart, 1922.

28 Cf. F. Naphtali, *Wirtschaftsdemodratie, ihr Wesen und Ziel* (*Economic Democracy – Its Essence and Aims*), Berlin, 1928, new edition, Frankfurt, 1966.

29 Cf. H. Everling, "Miteigentum und freie Gemeinwirtschaft" ("Co-Ownership and Free Commonweal Economy"), in *Gewerkschaftliche Monatshefte*, 7th year (1956), p. 728, et seq.

30 Cf. E. Grünfeld, "Das Genossenschaftswesen, volkswirtschaftlich und soziologisch betrachtet" ("The Cooperative Movement – from an Economic and Sociological Point of View"), in *Handbuch des Genossenschaftwesens*, Vol. I, Halberstadt, 1928.

31 Cf. G. Weisser, "Die Organisation in genossenschaftlichen Unternehmen" ("Organization in Cooperative Enterprises"), in *Annalen der Gemeinwirtschaft*, 32nd year, (1963) p.21 et seq.

32 Cf. H.G. Schachtschabel, "Genossenschaften III" ("Cooperatives III"), in *Handwörterbuch der Sozialwissenschaften* (*Dictionary of the Social Sciences*), Vol. 4, p. 388.

33 H.G. *Schachtschabel*, op. cit., p. 389.

34 Cf. H.G. Schachtschabel, op. cit., p. 388.

35 Cf. A. von Loesch, "Zur Geschichte der Arbeitnehmerbanken in Deutschland" ("The History of Workers' Banks in Germany"), in *Zeitfragen der Kreditwirtschaft*, Frankfurt, 1964, p. 179 et seq.

36 Cf. W. Hesselbach, "Funktion und Aufbau eines Bankensystems in Entwicklungsländern" ("Function and Establishment of a Banking System in Developing Countries"), "Vortrag auf einer Tagung der Friedrich-Ebert-Stiftung in Dakar". (Paper presented at a Meeting organized by the Friedrich-Ebert-Foundation at Dakar. In the proceedings, this text has been printed in French. German version in *Die öffentliche Wirtschaft* (*Journal of Public Economy*), Berlin, No. 4, vol. 17 (1968), p. 150.

37 Cf. R. Michels, *Die Psychologie der antikapitalistischen Massenbewegungen* (*The Psychology of Anti-Capitalist Mass-Movements*), Tübingen, 1926, p. 313.

38 R. Michels, op. cit., p. 313.

39 The poet Herwegh, as cited by E. Bloch, *Freiheit und Ordnung, Abriss der Sozialutopien* (*Freedom and Order – Sketch of Social Utopias*), New York, 1946, p. 135.

40 Cf. M. Weber, *Wirtschaft und Gesellschaft* (*Economy and Society*), 1st volume, 1st part, 3rd edition, Tübingen, 1947, p. 73.

41 Cf. H. Fuchs, "Der Begriff der Produktionsgenossenschaft und ihre Ideologie" ("The Concept of Producers' Society and its Ideology"), Dissertation, Cologne, 1927.

42 Cf. W. Abel, *Agrarpolitik* (*Agricultural Policy*), Göttingen, 1951, p. 88.

43 Cf. W. Engelhardt, "Produktivgenossenschaften" ("Producers' Societies"), in

Handwörterbuch der Sozialwissenschaften (*Dictionary of the Social Sciences*), Vol. 8, p. 611.

44 Cf. F. Oppenheimer, *Die Siedlungsgenossenschaft, Versuch einer positiven Uberwindung des Kommunismus durch Lösung des Genossenschaftsproblems und der Agrarfrage* (*The Cooperative Land-Settlement Society, an Attempt at a positive Victory over Communism through the Solution of the Cooperative Problem and of the Agrarian Question*), Leipzig, 1896, p. 45.

45 Cf. H. Crüger, "Produktivgenossenschaft" ("Producers' Cooperative Society"), in *Handwörterbuch der Staatswissenschaften* (*Dictionary of State Sciences*), 4th edition, Jena, 1925, Vol. 6, pp. 1128–1135 and H. Schulze-Delitzsch, *Schriften und Reden,* (*Writings and Discourses*), edited by F. Thorwart, Vol. I, Berlin, 1909–1913.

46 E. Bernstein, *Die Voraussetzungen des Sozialismus und die Aufgaben der Sozialdemokratie* (*The Conditions of Socialism and the Tasks of Social-Democracy*), Stuttgart, 1899, p. 97.

47 Cf. A. von Loesch, *Die Grenzen einer breiteren Vermögensbildung,* (*The Limits to a Wider Ownership of Capital*), Frankfurt, 1965, p. 97 et seq.

48 Cf. M. Weber, "Die protestantische Ethik und der Geist des Kapitalismus" "The Protestant Ethic and the Spirit of Capitalism"), *Gesammelte Aufsätze zur Religionssoziologie* (*Collected Papers on the Sociology of Religion*), Vol. I, Tübingen, 1920–1923.

49 Cf. F. Oppenheimer, op. cit., p. 126.

50 Cf. E. Bernstein, op. cit., p. 98.

51 Cf. J. Schumpeter, *Theorie der wirtschaftlichen Entwicklung; eine Untersuchung über Unternehmergewinn, Kapital, Zins und den Konjunkterzyklus* (*Theory of Economic Development. A Study of Entrepreneurial Profits, Capital, Interest and the Business Cycle*), Berlin, 1952.

52 Cf. F. von Wieser, "Grossbetrieb und Produktionsgenossenschaften" ("Large-Scale Enterprise and Producers' Cooperatives"), in *Gesammelte Abhandlungen* (*Collected Papers*), with a biographical introduction, edited by F.A. Hayek, Tübingen, 1929, pp. 288–289. Again cf. E. Paesch, *Die wirtschaftliche Bedeutung des kleingenossenschaftlichen Genossenschaftswesens* (*The Economic Importance of Cooperation Based upon Small Societies*), edited 1912, p. 113. Of a different opinion: H. Schulze-Delitzsch, "Arbeitende Klassen" ("Working Classes") p. 63, cf. F. von Wieser, op. cit. p. 275.

53 Cf. Webb-Potter, *Die britische Genossenschaftsbewegung* (*The British Cooperative Movement*), edited by L. Brentano, Leipzig, 1893, p. 114. Cf. also: v. Wieser, op. cit., p. 278 et seq.

54 Cf. W. Engelhardt, "Prinzipielle und aktuelle Aspekte der Produktivgenossenschaften", in *Sozialwissenschaft und Gesellschaftsgestaltung* ("Theoretical and Actual Aspects of Producers' Societies" in *Social Sciences and the Formation of Society*), Paper in Honour of Gerhard Weisser, Berlin, 1963, p. 439.

55 Cf. W.M. Kirsch, "Die Bedeutung des Genossenschaftswesens in unserer Zeit" ("The Importance of Cooperation in Our Times"), Paper presented to the Institut für Sozialpoltik und Arbeitsrecht eV (Institute for Social Policy and Labour Law) e.V. at Munich, 26.1.1960. Series of publications (*Schriftenreihe*) of this institute, 3rd series, booklet 11, p. 5.

56 Cf. W.M. Kirsch, "Europäische Marktintegration und Konsumgenossenschaften" ("European Market Integration and Consumers' Societies"), Paper presented to the 3rd International Congress of Consumers' Societies at Marburg, 1960. Published in the Proceedings of the Congress, edited by the Institute for Cooperation at the Philipps-University, Marburg, Göttingen, 1962, p. 145.

57 Cf. W. Astor, Artikel: "Eigenunternehmungen der Gewerkschaften" ("Enter-

prises of Trade Unions"), in *Internationales Handwörterbuch des Gewerkschaftswesens* (*International Manual of Trade Unionism*), Berlin, 1931, Vol. I, pp. 409–413.

58 Cf. W. Thiele and W. Göhring, *Ein halbes Jahrhundert Volksfürsorge. Werden und Wirken eines Versicherungsunternehmens* (*Half a century of 'Volksfürsorge'*. Origins and Activities of an Insurance Company), Darmstadt, 1962.

59 Cf. Chapter 9.

60 On the question of the commonweal function of consumers' cooperatives, see chapters 7 and 8.

61 Cf. E. Bernstein, *Die Voraussetzungen des Sozialismus und die Aufgaben der Sozialdemokratie* (*The Conditions of Socialism and the Tasks of Social-Democracy*) op. cit.

62 Cf. E. Bernstein, op. cit., p. 96.

63 Karl Marx, *Das Kapital* (*Capital*), Vol. 3, quoted from the new edition, Frankfurt, 1967, p. 456.

64 E. Bernstein, op. cit., p. 97.

65 E. Bernstein, op. cit., p. 97.

66 Cf. F. Lassalle, "Offenes Antwortschreiben an das Central-Comité zur Berufung eines Allgemeinen Deutschen Arbeiterkongresses zu Leipzig" ("Open Reply to the Central-Committee for Convening a General German Workers' Congress at Leipzig"), Zürich, 1863. Quoted from a reprint in *Ferdinand Lassalle, eine Auswahl für unsere Zeit* (*Ferdinand Lassalle, a Selection for Our Time*), edited by Helmut Hirsch, Frankfurt/Vienna/Zürich, 1963, p. 252/53.

67 F. Lassalle, op. cit., p. 253/54.

68 F. Lassalle, op. cit., p. 260.

69 G. Albrecht, *Sozialpolitik* (*Social Policy*), Göttingen, 1955, p. 52.

70 F. Lassalle, op. cit., p. 262.

71 Cf. V. Totomianz, "Genossenschaften" ("Cooperatives"), in *Internationales Handwörterbuch des Gewerkschaftswesens*, (*International Manual of Trade Unionism*), Vol. I, pp. 589–598.

72 E. Bernstein, op. cit., p. 117.

73 E. Bernstein, op. cit., p. 127.

74 E. Bernstein, op. cit., p. 139.

75 Cf. E. Bernstein, op. cit., p. 118.

76 We are here following W. Postelt "Elm, Adolf von", in *Internationales Handwörterbuch des Gewerkschaftswesens* (*International Manual of Trade Unionism*), Vol. I, p. 425.

77 Cf. the article "Fritz Naphtali" by Fritz Baade, in *Internationales Handwörterbuch des Gewerkschaftswesens*, op. cit., Vol. 2, p. 1136.

78 F. Naphtali, *Economic Democracy*, op. cit.

79 Cf. F. Naphtali, op. cit., p. 61 et seq.

80 Cf. F. Naphtali, op. cit., p. 81 et seq.

81 F. Naphtali, op. cit., pp. 99–100.

82 F. Naphtali, op. cit., p. 22.

83 Cf. W.M. Kirsch, "Die Bedeutung des Genossenschaftswesens in unserer Zeit" ("The Importance of Cooperation in Our Time"), paper submitted to the Institut für Sozialpolitik und Arbeitsrecht (Institute for Social Policy and Labour Law), Munich, 26th January, 1960. Series of Publications of this Institute, 3rd year, No. 11, p. 5.

84 Cf. W.M. Kirsch, op. cit., p. 6.

85 H. Faust, *Geschichte des Genossenschaftswesens, Ursprung und Weg der Genossenschaften im deutschen Sprachraum* (*History of Cooperation, Origin and Development of Cooperatives in the German Speaking Area*), Frankfurt, 1965.

86 H. Faust, op. cit., p. 357.
87 Cf. the paragraph "General Cooperative System", Chapter 2.
88 Cf. W.M. Kirsch, op. cit., p. 8.
89 Cf. V. Totmianz, op. cit., p. 594.
90 Cf. V. Totmianz, op. cit., p. 594.
91 Erich Batzer, "Starker Wandlungsprozess im Lebensmitteleinzelhandel" ("The Transformation of Food Retailing"), in *Wirtschaftskonjunktur (Business Cycles)*, Bulletin of the Institut für Wirtschaftsforschung (Institute for Business Research) Munich, Vol. 17, (1965), No. 4, pp. 33–41, see p. 33. The description of the situation in food retailing given in the above text largely follows Batzer's exposition.
92 Cf. Hans G. Schachtschabel, "Genossenschaften III" ("Cooperation III"), in *Handwörterbuch der Sozialwissenschaften* (*Dictionary of the Social Sciences*), p. 82.
93 Cf. W.M. Kirsch, op. cit., p. 9.
94 Cf. W.M. Kirsch, op. cit., p. 12.
95 See chapter 3.
96 Cf. G. Draheim, "Die Genossenschaft als Unternehmenstyp" ("The Cooperative as a Type of Enterprise"), Göttingen, 1954, and E. Boettcher, in "Gedanken zur Genossenschaftstheorie und Genossenschaftspraxis" ("Thoughts on Co-operative Theory and Co-operative Practice"), Papers presented on the occasion of the honorary doctorate granted to Prof. Draheim, 10th October, 1968, published by the Deutsche Genossenschaftskasse (German Cooperative Fund).
97 Cf. H.G. Schachtschabel, op. cit., p. 387.
98 Cf. W.M. Kirsch, "Europäische Marktintegration und Konsumgenossenschaften" ("Integration of the European Market and Consumers' Cooperatives"), discourse delivered at the Third International Congress of the Consumers' Cooperatives, Marburg, 1960, published in the Congress proceedings, and edited by the Institute for Cooperation at the Philipps University, Marburg; Göttingen, 1962, p. 145.
99 Cf. Fritz Werner, "Daseinsvorsorge und öffentliche Feuerversicherung – eine rechtsgeschichtliche Betrachtung" ("Provision for the Future and Public Fire Insurance – an Essay in the History of Law"), in *Ins dritte Jahrhundert, 200 Jahre hessische Brandversicherung* (*Into the Third Century – 200 years of Hessian Fire Insurance*), Kassel, 1967, p. 25–35.
100 Cf. W. Thiele and W. Göring, *Ein halbes Jahrhundert Voldsfürsorge – Werden und Wirken eines Versicherungsunternehmens* (*Half a Century of "Volksfürsorge" – Development and Activity of an Insurance Company*), published by the Management of "Alte Volksfürsorge", Darmstadt, 1962. The historical presentation follows this excellent biography of the firm in question.
101 Quoted according to W. Thiele and W. Göring, op. cit., p. 35.
102 Cf. *Handbuch der deutschen Gewerkschaftskongresse* (*Manual of German Trade Union Congresses*), prepared by Paul Barthe, Dresden, 1916, p. 454.
103 Cf. G. Wiegand, *Gemeinnützige Wohnungsunternehmen – Werden. Wesen, Widersacher,* (*Public Utility Housing Enterprises – Their Development, Character, and Adversaries*), Hamburg, 1962.
104 Cf. "Die Entwicklung des gewerkschaftlichen Wohnungsbaues" ("The development of Trade Union House Construction") in *Wir* (*We*), an information paper published by the "Neue Heimat", p. 15.
105 A. Vietor, in *Die Welt,* 27th April, 1967.
106 A Vietor, "Vom Wohnungsunternehmen zur Städtebau-Unternehmungsgruppe" ("From a House Building Enterprise to an Enterprise Group Constructing Entire Towns"), in *Neue Heimat, Monatshefte für neuzeitlichen Wohnungs – und Städtebau* (*Neue Heimat, Review of Modern Dwelling and Town Construction –*

a Monthly), 1970, No. 1, pp. 28/29.

107 ibid, p. 6.

108 This historical description follows the latest summary of this chapter of German banking history by Achim von Loesch, "Zur Geschichte der Arbeitnehmerbanken in Deutschland bis 1933" ("The History of Workers' Banks in Germany until 1933"), in *Zeitfragen der Kreditwirtschaft* (*Topical Questions on the Credit System*), Frankfurt, 1964, p. 179 seq. A bibliography is given there.

109 Cf. P. Barthel, *Handbuch der deutschen Gewerkschaftskongresse* (*Manual of German Trade Union Congresses*), Dresden, 1916, p. 135.

110 Cf. also Gerhard Neuenkirch, *Die Zusammenarbeit in der Gemeinwirtschaft* (*Collaboration in Commonweal Economy*), series of publications "Gemeinwirtschaft" of the "Bank für Gemeinwirtschaft" Frankfurt, No. 2, 1970, p. 21.

111 Cf. G. Neuenkirch, op. cit., p. 22.

112 Cf. G. Neuenkirch, op. cit., p. 24.

113 H.P. Dreitzel, "Uber die historische Methode in der Soziologie" ("The Historical Method in Sociology"), in *Sozialer Wandel – Zivilisation und Fortschritt als Kategorien der sozilogischen Theorie* (*Social Change – Civilization and Progress as Categories of Sociological Theory*), edited by H.D. Dreitzel, Neuwied/Berlin 1967, p. 450.

114 Cf. M. Weber, *Gesammelte Aufeätze zur Religionssoziologie* (*Collected Essays on the Sociology of Religion*), Vol. III, Tübingen, 1920–23.

115 Cf. M. Weber, *Wirtschaftsgeschichte,* (*Economic History*), Berlin, 1958.

116 In the context of this work the problematical nature of the profit motive in the framework of modern political economy cannot be examined. This has arisen since the "marginalist revolution" and the advent of the marginal utility school, by whom the principles of profit and utility maximization have been unjustifiably equated, a fact understandable only in terms of ideology. (Compare Hans Albert, "Erwerbsprinzip und Sozialstruktur" ("The Profit Motive and Social Structure"), in *Jahrbuch für Sozialwissenschaft,* Vol. 19 (1968), p. 1 et seq.

117 K. Oettle, "Die ökonomische Bedeutung der Rechtsform öffentlicher Betriebe" ("The Economic Importance of the Legal Form of Public Enterprises"), in *Archiv für öffentliche und freigemeinnützige Unternehmen,* Vol. 8 (1961), p. 197.

118 Cf. W. Eucken, *Die Grundlagen der Nationalökonomie* (*The Foundations of Economics*), 5th edition, Godesberg, 1947, p. 319 et seq.

119 W. Eucken, op. cit., p. 328.

120 W. Eucken, op. cit., p. 328.

121 O. v. Zwiedineck-Südenhorst, *Allgemeine Volkswirtschaftslehre* (*General Economics*), 1932, Introduction, quoted by W. Eucken, p. 330.

122 Cf. W. Eucken, op. cit., p. 332 et seq.

123 In reading these lines, we must not forget that the first edition of this book appeared in November, 1939. W. Eucken, op. cit. pp. 334–345.

124 G. Weisser. "Unternehmensmorphologie und Einzelwirtschaftspolitik als betriebswirtschaftliche Disziplinen der Sozialwissenschaften" ("Industrial Structure and the Policy of Individual Business Units in Industrial Economics Viewed from the Framework of the Social Sciences"), in *Archiv für öffentliche und freigemeinnützige Unternehmen,* Vol. 9 (1962), p. 17.

125 K. Oettle, op. cit., p. 224.

126 Cf. K. Oettle, op. cit., p. 216.

127 K. Oettle, op. cit., p. 200.

128 K. Oettle, op. cit., p. 214.

129 K. Oettle, op. cit., p. 216.

130 Cf. G. Weisser, "Die Lehre vom gemeinwirtschaftlichen Unternehmen" ("The Theory of Commonweal Enterprise"), in the journal *Archiv für öffentliche und*

freigemeinwirtschaftliche Unternehmen (*Archives for Public and Free Commonweal Enterprises*), Vol. I, 1954, p. 9.

131 ibid, p. 12.

132 ibid, p. 12.

133 G. Weisser, "Unternehmensmorphologie und Einzelwirtschaftspolitik als betriebswirtschaftliche Diszipinen der Sozialwissenschaften", op. cit., p. 6.

134 G. Weisser, "Die Lehre vom gemeinwirtschaftlichen Unternehmen", op. cit., p. 12.

135 G. Weisser, "Unternehmensmorphologie und Einzelwirtschaftspolitik als betriebswirtschaftliche Disziplinen der Sozialwissenschaften", op. cit., p. 6.

136 In these paragraphs I follow Professor Dr. Theo Thiemeyer's argument on the subject "commonweal economy", as presented in his paper for a course of the School of our Bank in the autumn 1968. (This paper has been printed in the meantime.)

137 Cf. Wilhelm Weber and Reimut Jochimsen, "Wohlstandsökonomik" ("Welfare Economics") in *Handwörterbuch der Sozialwissenschaften* ("*Dictionary of the Social Sciences*"), Vol. 12, pp. 346–359.

138 Cf. W. Rathenau, "Von kommenden Dingen" ("Of Things To Come"), in *Die neue Wirtschaft* (*The New Economy*), 1918.

139 Cf. W. Eucken, op. cit., p. 320 et seq.

140 Cf. G. Weisser, "Die Lehre von den gemeinwirtschaftlichen Unternehmen" ("The Theory of Commonweal Enterprise"), op. cit., p. 18.

141 Cf. R.G. Schachtschabel, "Ordnungspolitische Funktion der Genossenschaften" ("The Regulative Function of Cooperatives"), in the volume *"Genossenschaften und Genossenschaftsforschung"* ("*Cooperatives and Research on Cooperative Problems*"), publication in honour of Georg Draheim, Göttingen, 1968, p. 265 et seq. In chapter 17 of this volume the functions of cooperatives are set out in detail.

142 Cf. J.K. Galbraith, *"Die Moderne Industriegesellschaft"* (*"The New Industrial State"*), München/Zürich, 1968.

143 Cf. Th. Thiemeyer, op. cit.

144 Cf. J.A. Schumpeter, *Capitalism, Socialism and Democracy,* 2nd edition, München, 1950. p. 219 et seq.

145 J.A. Schumpeter, op. cit., p. 226.

146 Cf. J. Burnham, *Das Régime der Manager* (*The Managerial Revolution*), Stuttgart, 1948.

147 Cf. J.K. Galbraith, op. cit., p. 76 et seq.

148 Cf. J.A. Schumpeter, op. cit., p. 235 et seq.

149 Cf. L. v. Wiese, "Wettbewerb" ("Competition") in *Handwörterbuch der Sozialwissenschaften* (*Dictionary of the Social Sciences*), Vol. 12, p. 25.

150 Cf. L. v. Wiese, op. cit.

151 Cf. H. Arndt, *Schöpferischer Wettbewerb und klassenlose Gesellschaft* (*Creative Competition and the Classless Society*), Berlin, 1952, p. 45.

152 Cf. H. Ritschl, "Die Grundagen der Wirtschaftsordnung" ("The Foundations of Economic Order"), in *Gesammelte Aufsätze zur Lehre von der Wirtschaftsordnung* (*Collected Essays on the Theory of Economic Order*), Tübingen, 1954, p. 103.

153 Cf. B. Molitor, "Offentliche Wirtschaft und Privatisierung" ("Public Enterprise and Denationalization"), in *Hamburger Jahrbuch für Wirtschafts – und Gesellschaftspolitik,* Vol. 5, 1960, p. 78.

154 Cf. B. Molitor, op. cit., p. 79; H. Ritschl, "Offentliche Unternehmungen" ("Public Enterprise"), in *Handwörterbuch der Sozialwissenschaften* (*Dictionary of Social Sciences*), Vol. 10, p. 512.

155 H.G. Schachtschabel, "Ordnungspolitische Funktionen der Genossenschaften"

("Regulative Functions of Cooperatives"), op. cit., p. 277.

156 Cf. H.G. Schachtschabel, op. cit., p. 278.

157 "*Um die Zukunft des Volkswagenwerkes*" ("*The Future of the Volkswagen*"), Berlin, 1958, Vol. 6 of the series of publications (*Schriftenreihe*) of the "Gesellschaft für öffentliche Wirtschaft" (Society for Public Economy).

158 This was the fate of the Bundestag paper No. 145 (Motion of the deputy Deist and his colleagues). Cf. A. v. Loesch, "Die Stiftung Deutsches Volkswagenwerk als Instrument moderner Wirtschaftspolitik" ("The Foundation Voldswagen as an Instrument of Modern Economic Policy"), in *Archiv für öffentliche und freigemeinwirtschaftliche Unternehmungen,* Vol. 4. (1958), and "Volkswagen oder Volksaktien?" ("People's Cars or People's Shares?") in *Gerwerkschaftliche Monatshefte,* Vol. 9 (1958).

159 Cf. G. von Eynern, "Uber den Einfluss des Bundes auf seine Unternehmen" ("The Influence Exercised by the Federal Government on its Enterprises"), in *Hamburger Jahrbuch für Wirtschafts – und Gesellschaftspolitik,* Vol. 4 (1959), p. 115.

160 B. Molitor, op. cit., p. 80.

161 J.A. Schumpeter, *Kapitalismus, Sozialismus und Demokratie* (*Capitalism, Socialism and Democracy*), 2nd edition, Bern, 1950, p. 84.

162 H. Arndt, op. cit., p. 35.

163 H. Arndt, op. cit., p. 35 et seq.

164 Cf. J.A. Schumpeter, op. cit., pp. 82–83.

165 Cf. B. Molitor, op. cit., p. 86.

166 Cf. W. Zetzsche, "Die öffentlichen Unternehmen als Instrument der Konjunkturpolitik" ("Public Enterprises as Instruments of Business Cycle Policy"), in *Archiv für öffentliche und freigemeinwirtschaftliche Unternehmen,* Vol. 3 (1956), p. 97 et seq.

167 Cf. H. Ritschl, "Offentliche Unternehmungen", op. cit.

168 Cf. J.K. Galbraith, op. cit.

Index